the **chakra book**

OSHO

the **chakra book**

Energy and Healing Power of the Subtle Body

The text excerpts and meditations in this book are selected from various talks
by Osho given to a live audience. All of Osho's talks have been published in
full as books, and are also available as original audio recordings. Audio
recordings and the complete text archive can be found via the online OSHO
Library at www.osho.com/library

OSHO MEDIA INTERNATIONAL
New York • Zurich • Mumbai
an imprint of
OSHO INTERNATIONAL
www.osho.com/oshointernational

Distributed by Publishers Group Worldwide
www.pgw.com

Library of Congress Catalog-In-Publication Data is available

Printed in India by Manipal Technologies Limited, Karnataka

ISBN: 978-1-938755-95-8
This title is also available in eBook format ISBN: 978-0-88050-994-7

Contents

Introduction

Osho,
Is knowledge about esoteric subjects such as
chakras, collective unconsciousness, energy fields,
really helpful along the way, or not? Or will
whatever is needed come to me through
experience, in its own time?

Anything that is needed will come of its own accord, in its own
time. All this so-called esoteric knowledge about chakras,
energy fields, kundalini, astral bodies, is dangerous as knowledge.
As an experience, it is a totally different thing. Don't acquire it as
knowledge. If it is needed for your spiritual growth, it will come
to you in its right time, and then it will be an experience.

If you have an acquired knowledge, borrowed knowledge,
it is going to be a hindrance. For example Hindu Yoga believes
in seven chakras, Jaina scriptures mention nine chakras, and
Buddhist scriptures say that there are dozens of chakras and that

these are only the important ones which have been chosen by different schools. They don't give any fixed number. Acquired knowledge will be confusing: How many chakras? And what are you going to do with that knowledge, whether there are seven or nine or dozens? Your knowledge is not going to help; it can only hinder.

My own experience is that perhaps Buddha's experience is correct – and that does not make the Hindu Yoga or Jaina Yoga incorrect. Buddha is saying that there are energy fields, whirling energy fields, from the lowest point in your spine up to the very peak of your head. There are many; now it is only a question of a particular teaching which ones are important for it. That particular teaching will choose those. Hindus have chosen seven, Jainas have chosen nine. They don't contradict each other, it is simply that the emphasis is on whatever chakra the teaching feels to emphasize.

As far as I am concerned, you will come across only four chakras which are the most important.

One you know is your sex center. The second, just above it, which is not recognized in any Indian school of thought but has been recognized in Japan alone, is called the hara. It is between your navel and the sex center. The hara is the death chakra.

My own experience is that life, that is the sex center, and death, that is the hara, should be very close, and they are.

In Japan, when somebody commits suicide, it is called hara-kiri. Nowhere in the world does such a thing happen except in Japan. Suicide is committed everywhere, but with a knife? Just two inches below the navel, the Japanese forces a knife – and this is the most miraculous death; no blood, no pain – and death is instantaneous.

So the first chakra is the life chakra; it is a whirling energy. *Chakra* means wheel, moving. Just above the life chakra is the death chakra.

The third important chakra is the heart chakra. You can call it the love chakra, because between life and death the most important thing that can happen to a man or to a woman is love. And love has many manifestations: meditation is one of the manifestations of love, prayer is one of the manifestations of love. This is the third important chakra.

The fourth important chakra is what Hindu Yoga calls the *agna* chakra – just on your forehead between the two eyes. These four chakras are the most important.

The fourth is from where your energy moves beyond humanity into divinity. There is one more chakra, which is at the top part of your head, but you will not come across it in your life journey. That's why I am not counting it. After the fourth, you have transcended the body, the mind, the heart, all that is not you – only your being remains. And when death happens to such a person…

That's why in India the hara has not been taken note of; in the Hindu or Jaina or Buddhist Yoga, they were not considering people who commit suicide. They were thinking about people who were transforming their energy from the physical to the immaterial.

So the fifth chakra is the *sahasrar*. The Jainas count it, the Hindus count it – because a person who dies after transcending the fourth chakra… His energy, his being leaves the body, cracking the skull into two parts; that is the *sahasrar* chakra, but because it is not part of your life experience, I am not counting it. The four are your life experience. This one is the death of a person who is enlightened. He does not die from the hara.

That's why in India no school has taken note of the hara chakra. But in Japan they had to take note of it, because in Japan suicide was a form of etiquette.

You will be puzzled: the Japanese have such a totally different culture from the whole world; from small things to big things, they have their own approach.

I am reminded of one incident. A Japanese can commit suicide for small things because he cannot live a life of shame. If he feels ashamed, that is enough to finish his life – and you will not be able to conceive of what small things are thought so important that life is nothing.

A master, who was the greatest archer of Japan, was called by the king. The king wanted his son to become as great an archer as the master.

Now, it is Japanese etiquette that even when two people are going to fight with each other, first they will bow down to each other's divinity with folded hands, even though they are going to kill. Before killing, they will respect each other. So in ordinary life in Japan, you will find people everywhere bowing down to each other – on the road, in the restaurants. It is disappearing, as the modern Western influence is changing the whole world.

But the master archer was such an egoist that even in front of the king he waited: first the king should fold his hands, and then...

The king's court condemned the man and said, "You have committed such a shameful act. Just go back and commit hara-kiri." It was not such a big thing, but when the whole court had said it, the whole country would know about it.

The man went directly to his home and committed hara-kiri.

He had three hundred students. When they heard that their master had committed a shameful act, all three hundred students committed hara-kiri because it was so shameful that their master should have behaved like this.

Now this cannot happen anywhere else in the world. If the master had done something shameful – although it was not much of a shameful act, but even if it were, the students were completely innocent. But because they were the students of that master, it was enough to feel ashamed – they had followed such a man.

People have been committing hara-kiri in Japan for centuries. So when Buddhism reached there for the first time, about fourteen hundred years ago, and they started meditating, they were the first people to discover the hara center – because they had been using that center for centuries, so it was throbbing and vibrating and alive.

It all depends. In different cultures it may be a little different where the center is.

For example when Japanese started coming to me for sannyas, I was a little bit puzzled – because all over the whole world when you want to say yes, you move your head up and down. And the Japanese, when they want to say yes, move the head from side to side – which means no. All over the world, that is the sign for no – but that is their sign for yes, and the head moving up and down is their sign for no.

So when I would ask them something I would be very puzzled; I could not believe that they had come to take sannyas. They were sitting before me and I was asking, "Are you ready for sannyas?" and they would shake their heads. "Then why have you come? You have unnecessarily traveled here from Japan and you are sitting here in front of me just for that purpose, and you are saying no?"

Then my interpreter said to me, "You don't understand; that person is saying yes. In Japan, the head moving from side to side is yes; the head moving up and down is no." So you have to remember it when you are talking with the Japanese. Otherwise there is going to be great confusion – you will say something, they will understand something else. They cannot speak but they can understand.

In the Caucasus, where Gurdjieff was born, they have a system of chakras which is slightly different. It seems to be the difference between the people of the Caucasus and other people.

In India, three religions, Hinduism, Jainism and Buddhism, all have exactly the same points. They may count five or seven or nine, but the places are exactly the same. The centuries have affected their bodies in a different way.

In the Caucasus, there are thousands of people who are older than a hundred and fifty years. The Caucasus is the place with the oldest people in the whole world – and they are not old; at the age of one hundred and eighty, a person is still young. He is working on the farm just like any young man.

In the Caucasus, people always die while very young; they don't grow old. Naturally their bodies have developed in a different way. Their food has something to do with it, the climate, the geography, their land. It has created a different psychology.

Throughout the whole world, it is thought that seventy years is the time for everybody to die – that is the average; you can be five years earlier or five years later, but the average is seventy.

When George Bernard Shaw became seventy, he started looking in the small villages around London at the gravestones in their cemeteries, to see how long people in that village had lived. His friend said, "You are mad. Why are you wasting your time?"

He said, "I don't want to die at seventy. I have never been average in anything, and I cannot be average in death. So I am looking for a place where people don't believe that seventy is the average age to die, because that place will have a psychology of its own."

Finally he found a village where, on many stones in the graveyard, he found that it was written: This man lived one hundred and eight years, and died *untimely*.

He said, "This is the right place – where a man lives one hundred and eight years and still people think the poor fellow has died untimely, that it was not yet time to die."

After seventy years he moved from London – he had lived there for seventy years – to a village, after checking the cemetery. And he lived a hundred years. He proved that village had the psychology, that village had the vibe, that village had the idea that one hundred years is nothing.

When he would ask people if he could live to one hundred,

they would say, "One hundred is nothing; everybody lives to one hundred. You can go to the cemetery and see – one hundred and forty, one hundred and thirty; people live that long very easily. A hundred? – that is too early."

He lived one hundred years.

Certainly he proved one fact: that your psychology, your mind, your body, are impressed by the vibrations in which you live.

So you will come to experience chakras, you will come to experience energy fields, but it is better not to be knowledgeable because that is a difficult problem. You may read a book written five thousand years ago by a certain kind of person and you may not be of the same category. You may not find that chakra at the same place, and you will feel unnecessarily frustrated. And you will find a chakra in a place where the books don't mention it; then you will feel that you are abnormal, something is wrong with you. Nothing is wrong with you.

Energy fields, chakras, and all the esoteric things should be experienced. And keep your mind clean of all knowledge so that you don't have any expectation; wherever the experience happens, you are ready to accept it.

Each individual has differences, and differences come in such small things that you cannot conceive. For example, in the East, people sit on the floor. In cold countries, people cannot sit on the floor; a chair is absolutely necessary. Naturally their backbones, their spines will have a different shape than those of the people who sit on the floor, and their experiences of their kundalini will be different.

There are people who eat only once a day. For thousands of years they have never eaten more often than that. In South Africa there are tribes which eat only once in twenty-four hours. When they came across American missionaries, there was such laughter. "These idiots are eating five times a day! Breakfast – there is no fast at all and they are having 'break-fast.' And the whole day, something or other; and then coffee break, and tea break, and they go on… And in between they are chewing gum. These people have come to teach us religion and they are simply mad!"

In a way they are right, because they have beautiful bodies, they live longer, their bodies are not fat. Their bodies are like a deer's; they can run like deer – they have to because they are hunters. Their eyes are very clear, very perceptive; their bodies are very proportionate.

Now these people will have a totally different experience of their physiology. The meat eaters and the vegetarians will find differences to one another.

So it is better not to memorize from scriptures. Those scriptures are the experiences of certain people, of certain times, of certain circumstances; they were not written for you.

The scripture that is for you can be written only by you, by your own experience.

PART I

THE SEVEN CENTERS OF BEING

.

CHAPTER 1

The Changing Seasons of Life

Life has an inner pattern; it is good to understand it. Every seven years, physiologists say, the body and mind go through a crisis and a change. Every seven years all the cells of the body change, are completely renewed. In fact, if you live seventy years, the average limit, your body dies ten times. Each seventh year everything changes. It is just like changing seasons. In seventy years, the circle is complete. The line that moves from birth comes to death. The circle is complete in seventy years. It has ten divisions.

In fact, man's life should not be divided into childhood, youth, old age – that is not very scientific because every seven years a new age, a new step is taken.

For the first seven years a child is self-centered, as if he is the center of the whole world. The whole family moves around him. Whatever his needs are, they are to be fulfilled immediately, otherwise he will go into a tantrum: anger, rage… He lives like an emperor, a real emperor. His mother, his father – all are servants, and the whole family just exists for him. And of course he thinks the same is true for the wider world. The moon rises for him, the sun rises for him, the seasons change for him. A child remains absolutely egoistic, self-centered for seven years. If you ask psychologists they will say a child remains masturbatory for seven years, satisfied with himself. He does not need anything, anybody. He feels complete.

After seven years – a breakthrough. The child is no longer self-centered; he becomes eccentric, literally. *Eccentric* – the word means going out of the center. He moves toward others. The other becomes the important phenomenon – friends, gangs… Now he is not so interested in himself; he is interested in the other, the bigger world. He enters an adventure to know who this "other" Is. Inquiry starts.

After the seventh year, the child becomes a great questioner. He questions everything. He becomes a great skeptic because inquiry is there; he asks millions of questions. He bores the parents to death, he becomes a nuisance. He is interested in the other, and everything of the world is of interest. Why are the trees green? Why did God create the world? Why is this so? He starts becoming more philosophic; inquiry, skepticism – he insists on going into things.

He kills a butterfly to see what is inside, destroys a toy just to see how it works, throws a clock just to look into it, how it goes on ticking and chiming – what is the matter inside? He becomes interested in the other, but the other remains of the same sex. He is not interested in girls. If other boys are interested in girls, he will think they are sissy. Girls are not interested in boys. If some girl is interested in boys and plays with them, she is a tomboy, not normal, average; something is wrong. Psychoanalysts and psychologists will say this second stage is homosexual.

After the fourteenth year, a third door opens. He is no longer interested in boys, girls are no longer interested in girls. They are polite, but not interested. That's why any friendship that happens between the seventh year and the fourteenth is the deepest, because the mind is homosexual, and no longer in life will such friendship happen again. Those friends remain friends forever; it was such a deep tie. You will become friendly with people but it will remain acquaintance, not that deep phenomenon that happened between the seventh and the fourteenth year.

After the fourteenth year, a boy is not interested in boys. If everything goes normal, if he is not stuck somewhere, he will be interested in girls. Now he is becoming heterosexual – not only interested in the others, but really *the other*, because when a boy is interested in boys, the boy may be other but he is still a boy just like himself, not exactly the other. When a boy becomes interested in a girl, now he is really interested in the opposite, the real other. When a girl becomes interested in a boy, now the world enters.

The fourteenth year is a great revolutionary year. Sex becomes mature, one starts thinking in terms of sex, sex fantasies become prominent in the dreams. The boy becomes a great Don Juan, starts courting. Poetry arises, romance. He is entering the world.

By the twenty-first year – if everything goes normally, and a child is not forced by the society to do something which is not natural – by the twenty-first year, a child becomes interested more in ambition than in love. He wants a Rolls Royce, a great palace. He wants to be a success, a Rockefeller, a prime minister. Ambitions become prominent: desiring for the future, being a success. How to succeed, how to compete, how to move in the struggle is his whole concern.

Now he is not only entering the world of nature, he is entering the world of humanity, the marketplace. Now he is entering the world of madness. Now the market becomes the most prominent thing. His whole being goes toward the market: money, power, prestige.

If everything goes right – as it never goes, I am talking of the absolutely natural phenomenon – by the twenty-eighth year, a man is not in any way trying to enter an adventurous life. From twenty-one to twenty-eight, one lives in adventure; by the twenty-eighth year, one becomes more alert that not all desires can be fulfilled. There is more understanding that many desires are impossible. If you are a fool, you can go after them. But people who are intelligent, by the twenty-eighth year enter another door. They become more interested in security and comfort, less in adventure and ambition. They start settling. The twenty-eighth year is the end of hippiedom.

At twenty-eight, hippies become squares, revolutionaries are no longer revolutionaries; they start settling, they seek a comfortable life, a little bank balance. They don't want to be Rockefellers; finished, that urge is no longer there. They want a small house, but established, a cozy place to live in, security – so at least this much they can always have; a small bank balance. They go to the insurance company nearabout the age of twenty-eight. They start settling. Now the vagabond is no longer the vagabond. He purchases a house, starts living…he becomes civilized. The word *civilization* comes from the word *civis*, *citizen*. Now he becomes part of a town, a city, an establishment. He is no longer a vagabond, a wanderer. Now he is not going to Kathmandu and Goa. He is not going anywhere – finished, traveled enough, known enough; now he wants to settle and rest a little.

By the thirty-fifth year, life energy reaches its omega point. The circle is half complete and energies start declining. Now the man is not only interested in security and comfort, he becomes a Tory, orthodox. He becomes not only disinterested in revolution, he becomes an antirevolutionary. Now he is against all change. He is a conformist. He is against all revolution; he wants the status quo because now he has settled and if anything changes, the whole thing will unsettle. Now he is talking against hippies, against rebels; now he has become really a part of the establishment.

And this is natural. Unless something goes wrong, a man is not going to remain a hippie forever. That was a phase, good to pass through, but bad to be stuck in. That means you remain stuck at a certain stage. It was good to be homosexual between seven and fourteen, but if one remains homosexual for his whole life, that means he has not grown up, he is not adult. A woman has to be contacted, that is part of life. The other sex has to become important because only then will you be able to know the harmony of the opposites, the conflict, the misery, and the ecstasy: agony and ecstasy both. That is a training, a necessary training.

By the thirty-fifth year, one has become part of the conventional world. One starts believing in tradition, in the past, in the Vedas, the Koran, The Bible. One is absolutely against change because every change means your own life will be disturbed; now you have much to lose. You cannot be for revolution – you want to protect... One is for the law and the courts and the government. One is no longer an anarchist; one is all for the government, rules, regulations, discipline.

By the forty-second year, all sorts of physical and mental illnesses erupt because now life is declining. Energy is moving toward death.

Just as in the beginning energies were coming up and you were becoming more and more vital, energetic, you were becoming stronger and stronger – now just the opposite happens, you become weaker every day.

But your habits persist. You have been eating enough up to the age of thirty-five; now you continue your habit. You will start gathering fat. Now that much food is not needed. It was needed but now it is not needed because life is moving toward death, it does not need that much food. If you go on filling your belly as you were doing before, all sorts of illnesses will happen: high blood pressure, heart attack, insomnia, ulcers – they all happen nearabout forty-two. Forty-two is one of the most dangerous points. The hair starts falling out, becoming gray. Life is turning into death.

And near the age of forty-two, religion starts becoming important for the first time. You may have dabbled a little here and there in religion before, but now religion becomes important for the first time – because religion is deeply concerned with death. Now death is approaching and the first desire for religion arises.

Carl Gustav Jung has written that his whole life he has been observing that the people who come to him at the age of forty or nearabout are always in need of religion. If they go mad, neurotic, psychotic, they cannot be helped unless they become rooted in religion. They need religion; their basic need is religion. And if the society is secular and you have never been taught religion, the greatest difficulty comes nearabout the age of forty-two – because society does not give you any avenue, any door, any dimension.

Society was good when you were fourteen, because it gives enough of sex – the whole society is sexual; sex seems to be the only commodity hidden in every commodity. If you want to sell a ten-ton truck, you have to use a naked woman, or toothpaste – then too. Truck or toothpaste, it makes no difference: a naked woman is always smiling there behind. Really the *woman* is sold. The truck is not sold, the toothpaste is not sold; the woman is sold. And because the woman is there – her smile comes with the toothpaste – you have to purchase the toothpaste. Everywhere sex is sold.

So this society, a secular society, is good for young people. But they are not going to remain young forever. When they become forty-two suddenly the society leaves them in limbo. They don't know what to do now. They go neurotic because they don't know, they have never been trained, no discipline has been given them to face death. The society has made them ready for life, but nobody has taught them to become ready for death. They need as much education for death as they need for life.

If I was allowed my way, I would divide universities into two parts: one for young people, another for old people. Young people would come to learn the art of life – sex, ambition, struggle. Then when they became old and reached the forty-two mark, they would come back to the university to learn about death, God, meditation – because then the old universities wouldn't be of any help to them. They need a new training, a new discipline, so that they can become anchored with the new phase that is happening to them.

This society leaves them in limbo; that's why in the West there is so much mental illness. It is not so much in the East. Why? – because the East still gives a little training in religion. It has not disappeared completely; howsoever false, pseudo, it is still there, it exists, just around the corner. No longer in the marketplace, no longer in the thick of life, just at the side, but there is a temple. Out of the way of life, but still it is there. You have to walk a few steps and you can go there. It still exists.

In the West religion is no longer part of life. Nearabout the age of forty-two, every Westerner is going through psychic problems. Thousands of types of neuroses happen – and ulcers. Ulcers are the footprints of ambition. An ambitious man is bound to have ulcers in the stomach: ambition bites, it eats itself. An ulcer is nothing but eating yourself. You are so tense that you have started eating your own stomach lining. You are so tense, your stomach is so tense, it never relaxes. Whenever the mind is tense, the stomach is tense. Ulcers are the footprints of ambition. If you have ulcers, that shows you are a very successful man.

If you have no ulcers, you are a poor man: your life has been a failure, you failed utterly. If you have your first heart attack nearabout forty-two, you are a great success: you must be at least a cabinet minister, or a rich industrialist, or a famous actor; otherwise, how will you explain the heart attack? A heart attack is the definition of success. All successful people will have heart attacks. They have to.

The whole system is burdened with toxic elements: ambition, desire, future, tomorrow – which are never there. You lived in dreams. Now your system cannot tolerate it anymore. You remain so tense for the future that tension has become your very style of life. Now it is a deep-rooted habit.

At forty-two, again a breakthrough comes. One starts thinking about religion, the other world. Then life seems to be very short. Little time is left. How can you achieve God, nirvana, enlightenment? Hence the theory of reincarnation: don't be afraid, again you will be born, again and again, and the wheel of life will go on moving and moving. Don't be afraid: there is enough time, there is enough eternity left – you can attain.

That's why in India three religions were born – Jainism, Buddhism and Hinduism – and they don't agree on any other point except reincarnation. They don't agree on any other point. Even about such an important theory as God there is not an agreement. Jainas say there is no God, Buddhists say there is no God. Even about a more important theory than God, the theory of the soul, atman – Buddhists say there is no atman, no soul. Such divergent theories! Not even agreeing on the basic foundations: God, self… But they all agree on the theory of reincarnation. There must be something to it.

They all need time, because to attain *brahman* – Hindus call it *brahman* – much time is needed. It is such a great ambition, and at the age of forty-two, you become interested. Only twenty-eight years are left.

And this is just the beginning of the interest. In fact, at the age of forty-two, you become again a child in the world of religion. Only twenty-eight years are left. Time seems too short, not enough at all to attain such great heights – *brahman*, Hindus call it. Jainas call it *moksha*, absolute freedom from all past karmas. Thousands and millions of lives have been there in the past; how are you going to cope within twenty-eight years? How will you undo the whole past? Such a vast past is there – bad and good karmas. How are you going to clean your sins completely within twenty-eight years? It seems unjust. God is demanding too much, it is not possible. You will feel frustrated if only twenty-eight years are given to you.

And Buddhists – who don't believe in God, don't believe in

the soul – also believe in reincarnation, nirvana, the final emptiness, the total emptiness. When you have remained filled with so
much rubbish for so many lives, how are you going to unburden
within twenty-eight years? It is too much, seems an impossible
task. They all agree on one thing, that more future is needed,
more time is needed.

Whenever you have ambition, time is needed. And to me, a
religious person is one who does not need time. He is liberated
here and now, he achieves to *brahman* here and now, he is *mukta*,
liberated, enlightened here and now. A religious man does not
need time at all because religion happens in a timeless moment.
It happens now, it always happens now. It has never happened
otherwise, in no other way has it ever happened.

At the age of forty-two, the first urge arises, vague, not clear,
confused. You are not even aware of what is happening, but you
start looking at the temple with keen interest. Sometimes, by the
way, as a casual visitor, you come to the church also. Sometimes,
having time, not doing anything, you start looking in The Bible
which has always been gathering dust on the table. Vague, not
exactly clear, just like the small child who is vague about sex
starts playing with his own sex organ, not knowing what he is
doing. A vague urge… Sometimes one sits alone silently, suddenly feels peaceful, not knowing what he is doing. Sometimes
one starts a mantra heard in the childhood. The old grand-
mother used to do it; feeling tense, one starts repeating it. One
starts seeking, searching for a guru, somebody to guide you.
One takes initiation, starts learning a mantra, repeating it sometimes, then again forgetting for a few days, again repeating… A
vague search, groping…

By the forty-ninth year, the search becomes clear; seven
years it takes for the search to become clear. Now a determina-
tion arises. You are no longer interested in the others, particularly if everything has gone right – and I have to repeat this again
and again because it never goes right. At the age of forty-nine,

one becomes disinterested in women. A woman becomes disinterested in man – the menopause, the forty-ninth year… The man doesn't feel like being sexual. The whole thing looks a little juvenile, the whole thing looks a little immature.

But society can force… In the East, they have been against sex and they have suppressed sex. When a boy is fourteen they are suppressing sex, and they want to believe that he is still a child: he doesn't think about girls. Other boys maybe – they always belong to the neighborhood, never your boy; he is innocent, like a child, like an angel. And he *looks* very innocent, but that's not true: he fantasizes. The girl has entered his consciousness, has to enter – it is natural – and he has to hide it. He starts masturbating, and he has to hide it. He has wet dreams and he has to hide it.

In the East, a boy of fourteen becomes guilty. Something wrong is happening – only to him, because he cannot know that everybody everywhere is doing the same. And much is expected of him – that he should remain an angel, a virgin, not thinking about girls, not even dreaming about girls. But he has become interested and society is suppressing.

In the West, this suppression has disappeared, but another has come – and this has to be understood, because it is my feeling that the society can never be non-suppressive. If it changes one suppression, immediately it starts another. Now the next suppression is near the age of forty-nine in the West: people are forced to remain in sex because the whole teaching says, "What are you doing? – a man can be sexually potent up to the age of ninety!" Great authorities are saying it. And if you are not potent, and you are not interested, you start feeling guilty. At the age of forty-nine, a man starts feeling guilty that he is not making as much love as he should.

There are teachers who go on teaching: "This is nonsense. You can make love, you can make love up to the age of ninety. Go on making love." And they say if you don't make love you will lose potency. If you continue, then your organs continue functioning. If you stop, then they will stop. And once you stop sex, life energy will drop down, you will die soon.

If the husband stops, the wife is after him: "What are you doing?" If the wife stops the husband is after her: "This is against the psychologists and may create some perversion!"

In the East, we did one stupidity, and in the West also in the ancient days they did the same. It was against religion for a child of fourteen to become sexually potent – and he becomes so naturally. The child cannot do anything, it is beyond his control. What can he do? How can he do it? And all teaching about *brahmacharya* at the age of fourteen is stupid. You are suppressing. But the old authorities, traditions, gurus, *rishis*, old psychologists and religious people – they were all against, the whole authority was against. A child was suppressed. Guilt was created. Nature was not allowed.

Now just the opposite is happening at the other end. At the age of forty-nine, psychologists are forcing people to continue to make love; otherwise you will lose life. And at the age of forty-nine… As at the age of fourteen sex naturally arises, so at the age of forty-nine it naturally subsides. It has to, because every circle has to be complete.

That's why in India we had decided that at the age of fifty man should start becoming a *vanprasth*, his eyes should move toward the forest, his back toward the marketplace. *Vanprasth* is a beautiful word; it means one who starts looking toward the Himalayas, toward the forest. Now his back is toward life and ambitions and desires and all that. Finished. He starts moving toward aloneness, toward being himself.

Before this, life was too much and he could not be alone; there were responsibilities to be fulfilled, children to be raised. Now they have become young people. They are married – by the time you are forty-nine your children are getting married, set-tling. They are no longer hippies, they must be reaching the age of twenty-eight. They will settle – now you can unsettle. Now you can move beyond the home; you can become homeless. At the age of forty-nine, one should start looking toward the forest, moving inward, becoming introvert, becoming more and more meditative and prayerful.

At the age of fifty-six, again a change comes, a revolution. Now it is not enough to look toward the Himalayas, one has to really travel, one has to go. Life is ending, death is coming nearer. At the age of forty-nine one becomes disinterested in the other sex. At the age of fifty-six one should become uninterested in others, society, social formalities, the club – Rotary and Lions. At the age of fifty-six, one should resign from all Rotaries, all Lions; it looks foolish now, childish. Go to some Rotary Club or Lions Club and see people, dressed up with their ties and everything. It looks juvenile, childish; what are they doing? Lions – the very name looks foolish. For a small child, good. Now they have for small children Cub clubs, and for women Lioness clubs. For cubs, perfectly right, but for lions and lionesses…? It shows that the minds are mediocre. They have no intelligence, nothing at all.

At the age of fifty-six, one should be so mature as to come out of all social entanglements. Finished! One lived enough, learned enough; now one gives thanks to everybody and comes out of it. Fifty-six is the time one should naturally become a sannyasin. One should take sannyas, one should renounce. It is natural – as you enter, so you should renounce. Life should have an entrance and it should also have an exit; otherwise it will be suffocating. You enter and you never come out and then you say you are suffocated, in agony.

There *is* an exit, and that is sannyas. You come out. You are not even interested in others by the age of fifty-six.

By the age of sixty-three you again become like a child, only interested in yourself. That is what meditation is – to be moving inward, as if everything has fallen away. Only you exist. Again you have become a child – of course, very much enriched by life, very mature, understanding, with great intelligence. Now you again become innocent. You start moving inward. Only seven years are left, and you have to prepare for death. You have to be ready to die. And what is the readiness to die?

To die celebrating is the readiness to die. To die happy, joyfully, to die willingly, welcomingly, is to be ready. Existence gave you an opportunity to learn, and be, and you learned. Now you would like to rest. Now you would like to go to the ultimate home.

It was a sojourn. You wandered in a strange land, you lived with strange people, you loved strangers, and you learned much. Now the time has come: the prince must return to his own kingdom.

Sixty-three is the time when one becomes completely enclosed in one's self. The whole energy moves in and in and in, turning in. You become a circle of energy, not moving anywhere. No reading, not much talking. More and more silent, more and more with one's self, remaining totally independent of all that is around you. The energy by and by subsides.

By the age of seventy, you are ready. And if you have followed this natural pattern, just before your death, nine months before your death, you will become aware of it. As a child has to pass nine months in the mother's womb, the same circle is totally repeated, completely repeated, utterly repeated. By the time death comes, nine months before, you will become aware. Now you are entering the womb again. This womb is no longer outside in the mother, this womb is inside you.

Indians call the innermost shrine of a temple the *garbha*, the womb. When you go to a temple, the innermost part of the temple is called the womb. It is very symbolically called so, very consideredly; it is the womb one has to enter. In the last phase – nine months – one enters oneself, one's own body becomes the womb. One moves to the innermost shrine where the flame has always been burning, where the light has always been, where the temple is, where the god has always been living.

This is the natural process. For this natural process no future is needed. You have to be living naturally *this* moment. The next moment will come out of it on its own accord – as a child grows and becomes a youth. There is no need to plan for it, one simply becomes; it is natural, it happens. As a river flows and comes to the ocean, the same way you flow, and you come to the final, the ocean. But one should remain natural, floating, and in the moment. Once you start thinking about the future and ambition and desire, you are missing this moment. And this moment missed will create perversion because you will always lack something; there will be a gap.

If a child has not lived his childhood well, that unlived childhood will enter his youth – because where will it go? It has to be lived. And when a child is at the age of four and dances and jumps and runs around, butterfly-catching, it is beautiful. But when a young man of twenty runs after butterflies he is crazy. Then you have to admit him to the hospital; he is a mental case. Nothing was wrong with it at the age of four; it was just natural, it was the thing to do. It was the *right* thing to do; if the child was not running after butterflies something was wrong, he had to be taken to the psychoanalyst.

Then it was okay; but when he is twenty and running after butterflies, you should suspect something has gone wrong, he has not grown up. The body has grown, the mind is lagging behind. It must be somewhere in his childhood – he was not allowed to live it completely. If he lives childhood completely, he will become a young man: beautiful, fresh, uncontaminated by the childhood. He will shed childhood as a snake sheds its old skin. He will come out of it fresh. He will have the intelligence of a young man, and he won't look retarded.

Live youth completely. Don't listen to the Eastern and ancient authorities. Just drop them out of the way. If you meet them on the way, kill them immediately. Don't listen to them because they have killed youth, they are suppressive of youth. They are against sex, and if a society is against sex, sex will spread all over your life. It will become poison. Live it! Enjoy it!

Between the fourteenth and twenty-first year, a boy is at his highest peak of sexuality. In fact, near the age of seventeen or eighteen he reaches the peak of sexuality. Never will he be so potent. And if those moments are missed he will never achieve the beautiful orgasm that could have been achieved near the age of seventeen or eighteen.

I am in a continuous difficulty because society forces you to remain celibate, at least up to the twenty-first year. That means the greatest possibility of achieving sex, learning sex, entering sex, will be missed. By the time you reach twenty-one, twenty-two, you are already old as far as sex is concerned! Near the age of seventeen you were at the peak – so potent, so powerful, that the orgasm, the sexual orgasm, would have spread to your very cells. Your whole body would have taken a bath of eternal bliss.

And when I say sex can become *samadhi*, I don't say it for people who are seventy, remember. I am saying it for people who are seventeen. Old men come to me and they say, "We have read your book, *From Sex to Superconsciousness*, but we never achieve anything like this."

How can you achieve it? You have missed the time, and it cannot be replaced. And I am not responsible; society is responsible, and you listened to it.

If between the ages of fourteen and twenty-one a child is allowed to have free sex, absolutely free sex, he will never bother about sex. He will be completely free. He will not look at the magazines *Playboy* and *Playgirl*. He will not hide nude, ugly, obscene pictures in the cupboard or in The Bible. He will not go out of his way to throw things at women. He will not become a bottom-pincher. These things are ugly, simply ugly, but you go on tolerating them and not feeling what is happening, why everybody is neurotic.

Once you find a chance to rub against a woman's body, you

never miss it. What ugliness! – rubbing against a body. Something has remained unfulfilled in you. And when an old man looks with lustful eyes, there is nothing like that; it is the ugliest thing in the world when an old man looks with lust in his eyes. His eyes should be innocent now, he must be finished by now. Not that sex is something ugly; remember, I am not saying sex is ugly. Sex is beautiful at its own time and season, and it is ugly out of season, out of time. Sex is a disease when it is in a ninety-year-old man. That's why people say "dirty old man." It *is* dirty.

A young man is beautiful, sexual. He shows vitality, life. An old man, sexual, shows an unlived life, an empty life, immature. He missed the opportunity and now he cannot do anything, but he goes on thinking, rambling in the mind about sex, fantasizing.

Remember, between the fourteenth and the twenty-first year, a right society will allow absolute freedom for sex. And then society will become less sexual automatically. Beyond this time there will be no sex; the disease will not be there. Live it when the moment is ripe and forget it when the moment has gone. But that you can do only if you have lived; otherwise you cannot forget and you cannot forgive. You will cling, it will become a wound inside.

In the East, don't listen to the authorities, whatever they say. Listen to nature. When nature says it is time to love, love. When nature says it is time to renounce, renounce. And don't listen to the foolish psychoanalysts and psychologists in the West. Howsoever refined instruments they have – Masters and Johnson and others – and however many vaginas they have been testing and examining, they don't know life.

In fact, I suspect that these Masters and Johnsons and Kinseys in the West are voyeurs. They themselves are ill about sex; otherwise who bothers to watch one thousand vaginas with instruments – watching what is happening inside when a woman makes love? Who bothers? What nonsense! But when things become perverted, this type of thing happens. Now Masters and Johnsons have become the experts, the final authorities. If you are having any sexual problem, they are the final authority to go to. And I suspect they have missed their youth, they have not lived their sex lives rightly. Somewhere something is lacking and they are fulfilling it through such tricks.

And when a thing is in the garb of science you can do anything. Now they have made false, electric penises, and those electric penises go on throbbing in the real vaginas, and they go on trying to find what is happening inside, whether orgasm is clitoral or vaginal, what hormones are flowing, what hormones are not flowing, and how long a woman can make love. They say: to the very end. A woman can make love on her deathbed.

In fact, their suggestion is that after menopause a woman can make better love than ever – that means after the forty-ninth year. Why do they say that? – because, they say, before the forty-ninth a woman is always afraid of getting pregnant. Even if she is on the pill, no pill is a hundred percent proof; there is a fear. By the forty-ninth year, when the menopause comes and the period stops, then there is no fear; a woman is completely free.

If their teaching spreads women are going to become vampires, and old women will chase men because they are unafraid and the authority sanctions it. In fact, they say that then is the right time to enjoy – without any responsibility. For men also they go on saying the same. And they have come across men – so now they say there is no average – they have come across a man who in his sixtieth year can make love five times a day. This man seems to be a freak. Something is wrong with his hormones and his body. And at the age of sixty! He is not natural, because as I see it – and this I am saying out of my own experiences in many lives, I can remember them – by the forty-ninth year a natural man is not interested in women; the interest goes. As it comes, it goes.

Everything that comes has to go. Everything that arises has to fall. Every wave that arises has to disappear. There must be a time when it goes. At fourteen it comes; at forty-nine or nearabout it goes.

But a man making love five times a day at the age of sixty –
something is wrong, something is very, very wrong. His body is
not functioning rightly. It is the other end of impotence, the
other extreme. When a boy of fourteen does not feel any sex, a
young man of eighteen has no desire, something is wrong – he
has to be treated. When a man of sixty needs to make love five
times a day, something is wrong. His body has gone berserk. It is
not functioning rightly, naturally.

If you live in the moment totally, then there is no need to
worry for the future. A rightly lived childhood brings you to a
right, ripe youth – flowing, vital, alive, a wild ocean of energy. A
rightly lived youth brings you to the very settled calm and quiet
life. A calm and quiet life brings you to a religious inquiry: What
is life? Living is not enough, one has to penetrate the mystery. A
calm and quiet life brings you to meditative moments. Meditation
brings you to renounce all that is useless now, just junk, garbage.
The whole of life becomes garbage; only one thing remains always
eternally valuable, and that is your awareness.

By the time of the seventieth year, when you are ready to die
– if you lived everything rightly, in the moment, never post-
poning for the future, never dreaming for the future, you lived in
the moment totally, whatsoever it was – nine months before your
death you will become aware… You have attained that much
awareness, you can see: now death is coming.

Many saints have declared their deaths, but I have not come
across a single instance when the death was declared earlier than
nine months. Exactly nine months before, a man of awareness,
uncluttered with the past – because one who never thinks of
the future will never think of the past. They are together, the past
and future are together, joined together. When you think of the
future, it is nothing but the projection of the past; when you think
of the past, it is nothing but trying to plan for the future. They are
together. The present is out of them. A man who lives in this
moment now and here is not cluttered with the past and not

cluttered with the future. He remains unburdened. He has no burden to carry, he moves without weight. Gravitation doesn't affect him. In fact, he doesn't walk, he flies. He has wings.

Before he dies, exactly nine months before, he will become aware that death is coming. And he will enjoy and he will celebrate and he will tell people, "My ship is coming, and I am only on this bank a little while more. Soon I will be going to my home. This life has been beautiful, a strange experience. I loved, learned, lived much, I am enriched. I had come here with nothing and I am going with much experience, much maturity."

He will be thankful to all that has happened – both good and bad, both right and wrong both, because he learned from *everything*, not only from right, from wrong also. Sages that he came across, he learned from them; and sinners, yes, from them also – they all helped. People who robbed him helped, people who helped him helped; people who were friends helped, people who were enemies helped. Everything helped. Summer and winter, satiety and hunger, everything helped. One can be thankful to all.

When one is thankful to all, and ready to die celebrating for this opportunity that was there, death becomes beautiful. Then death is not the enemy, it is the greatest friend, because it is the crescendo of life. It is the highest peak that life achieves. It is not the end of life, it is the climax. It looks like the end because you have never known life. To one who has known life it appears as the very crescendo, the very peak, the highest peak.

Death is the culmination, the fulfillment. Life does not end in it; in fact, life flowers in it, it *is* the flower. But to know the beauty of death, one has to be ready for it, one has to learn the art. That's why I go on saying that I am here to teach you how to die. A master is a death. He allows you to die in him. He helps you to die every moment to the past, and he helps you to live an uncluttered moment – this moment.

CHAPTER 2

Man Is a Rainbow

Man is a rainbow, all the seven colors together. That is his beauty and that is his problem too. Man is multifaceted, multidimensional. His being is not simple, it is a great complexity. And out of that complexity is born the harmony we call God: the divine melody.

So the first thing to be understood about man is that man is not yet. Man is only a possibility, a potentiality. Man can be, man is a promise. The dog is, the rock is, the sun is – man *can be*. Hence the anxiety and anguish. One can miss too; there is no certainty. You may flower, you may not flower. Hence the shivering, the shaking, the trembling inside: "Who knows whether I will be able to do it or not?"

Man is a bridge between the animal and the divine. The animals are tremendously happy – of course not aware, not *consciously* happy, but tremendously happy, unworried, non-neurotic. God is tremendously happy and conscious. Man is just in between the two, in limbo, always wavering – to be or not to be?

Man is a rainbow, I say, because a rainbow will give you the total perspective in which man can be understood – from the lowest to the highest. The rainbow has seven colors, man has seven centers of his being. The allegory of the seven is very ancient. In India, the allegory has taken the form of seven chakras: the lowest is *muladhar* and the highest is *sahasrar* and between these two are five steps, five more chakras. And man has to pass through all seven chakras – seven steps toward the divine.

Ordinarily, we are stuck at the lowest. The first three – *muladhar*, *svadhishthan* and *manipura* – are animal chakras. If you live in the first three, you are no different to the animals – and then you are committing a crime. Not that you are actually committing a crime – you are committing a crime because you will not be able to be what you were meant to be; you will miss the possibility. If a seed does not grow to be a flower, it has committed a crime – against nobody; against himself. And the sin that one commits against oneself is the greatest. In fact, we commit sins toward others only when we have committed the first, fundamental sin against ourselves.

The first three chakras are concerned with food, money, power, domination, sex. Food is the lowest, sex is the highest, in the lowest three chakras. This has to be understood. Food is the lowest – a food-obsessed person is in the lowest category of animals. He simply wants to survive. He has no purpose, he just wants to survive for survival's sake. If you ask him for what, he has no answer to give to you.

One day, Mulla Nasruddin told me, "I wish I had more land."

I asked him, "But why? As it is, you have enough."

He said, "I could raise a lot more cows."

I asked him, "And what would you do with them?"

He said, "Sell them and make money."

"And then? Then what you are going to do with that money?"

"Buy more land."
And I asked him, "For what?"
"To raise a lot more cows."

This way it goes, just a vicious circle in which you never come out: you eat to live, you live to eat. This is the lowest possibility. The lowest form of life is the amoeba. The amoeba simply eats, that's all. An amoeba has no sex life, an amoeba goes on eating whatsoever is available – the amoeba is exactly the symbol of the lowest man. The amoeba has no other organs, only the mouth; his whole body functions as a mouth. He goes on digesting whatsoever comes close by; whatsoever comes close, he simply digests it. He absorbs it with his whole body; his whole body is a mouth. He becomes more and more, bigger and bigger; then comes a point where he is too big and he cannot manage – then he splits in two. Then there are two amoebas instead of one; then they start doing the same thing. The amoeba simply eats and lives, and lives to eat more.

A few people live at this lowest level. Beware of it – life has something more to give to you. It is not just survival, it is survival for something significant. Survival is necessary but is not the end unto itself; it is just a means.

The second type, a little higher than the food-obsessed, is the power-maniac, the politician. He wants to dominate people. For what? He feels very, very inferior deep inside: he wants to show to the world: "I am somebody; I can dominate, I can put you in your right place." He has not put himself in *his* right place and he tries to put the whole world in *its* place. He is the ego-obsessed person. He can move in any direction: if he moves into money, he will go on hoarding money – money becomes the power symbol. If he moves into politics, he cannot contain himself until he has reached the very end – and there is nothing.

The real man tries to conquer himself, not others. He wants to know himself. He does not want to fulfill some inner gap by dominating somebody else. The real man loves freedom for himself and for others too.

Third is sex – and I say it is better than food, than politics, because it has a little higher quality: it shares. It has something higher. In food, you simply absorb; you don't share. In domination, you destroy; you don't create. Sex is the highest possibility on the lower plane – you share, you share your energy, and you become creative. As far as animal existence is concerned, sex is the highest value. And people are stuck somewhere with these three.

The fourth is the *anahata* chakra. The first three are animal, the last three are divine, and in between these two is the fourth, *anahata* – the heart chakra, the lotus of the heart, the chakra of love. And that is the bridge. Love is the bridge between the animal and the divine. Try to understand it as deeply as possible. Below the heart, a man is animal; above the heart, he becomes divine. Only in the heart is a man human. That's why a man who can feel, who can love, who can pray, who can cry, who can laugh, who can share, who can have compassion, is the real human being. Humanity has dawned in him, the first rays of the sun have entered in him.

Then fifth is *vishuddha*, sixth is *agya*, and seventh is *sahasrar*. With the fifth, love becomes more and more meditative, more and more prayerful. With the sixth, love is no longer a relationship. It is not even a prayer – it has become a state of being. It is not that you love somebody, no. Now it is something like *you are* love. It is not a question of loving – your very energy is love. You cannot do otherwise. Now love is the natural flow – just as you breathe, so you love; it is an unconditional state. And with the seventh is *samadhi, sahasrar*: you have arrived home.

In Christian theology, you can find the same allegory in the story that God created the world in six days and on the seventh day he rested. Those six days are the six chakras – the six centers of being. The seventh is rest: one has arrived home, one rests.

That allegory has not been understood well. Christians, and particularly Christian theologians, never go very deep. Their understanding remains superficial – at the most, logical, theoretical, but it never touches the real point. God created the world: first he created matter, and last he created man. For five days he was creating everything else in the world – matter, animals, birds – then on the sixth day he created man. And in the last moment of the sixth day he created woman. Now this is very symbolic: woman is the last creation – even man is not the last. And the allegory is still more beautiful because it says he created woman out of man. That means woman is a refinement of man, a more purified form.

First: a woman means intuition, poetry, imagination. Man means will, prose, logic, reason. These are symbols: man means an aggressive quality, woman means receptivity. Receptivity is the highest. Man means logic, reasoning. analysis, philosophy; woman means religion, poetry, imagination – more fluid, more flexible. Man is fighting with God. Science is purely a male by-product – man fighting, struggling, trying to conquer. Woman never fights; she simply welcomes, she waits, she surrenders.

And the Christian allegory says God created man first. Man is the highest in the animal kingdom – but as far as humanity is concerned, woman is higher. Christian theologians have interpreted it in an absolutely wrong way – they have interpreted in a male chauvinist way. They think man is more important, so God created man first. Then animals must be even more important! The logic is false. They think man is the real thing, woman is just an appendix. At the last moment, God felt that something was missing so he took one bone out of man and created the woman. Woman is not to be thought very significant – just a helpmate, just so that man feels good, otherwise he will be alone. The story is analyzed in such a way that it seems that woman is less important than man – just a toy for man to play with, otherwise he will be alone. God loved man so much that he thought he would be sad and lonely. No, this is not true.

Imagination comes only when the will is surrendered. The same energy that is will becomes imagination, and the same energy that becomes aggression becomes reception, and the same energy that fights becomes cooperation. The same energy that is anger becomes compassion. Compassion comes out of anger; it is a refinement of anger, it is a higher symphony out of anger. Love arises out of sex; it is a higher reach, more purified.

God created woman after he created man because woman can be created only afterward. First you have to create the crude energy and then you can refine it. The refinement cannot come first. And in this allegory there is a message – that every man has to become feminine before he reaches to the seventh. This is at the sixth center. In yoga, the sixth center is called *agya* chakra – it means the center of will. *Agya* means order, commandment. It is the most powerful center, the sixth, and many become stuck there. Then they go on playing with spiritual energies and go on doing foolish things. At the sixth center, man has to turn into a woman and his whole will has to be used for only one thing – that is, he has to will surrender. To will surrender is the greatest thing in the world; and this can be done only if you have willpower – not ordinary, *extraordinary* willpower.

Ordinarily, you think people who surrender are weaklings – you are wrong. Only very strong people can surrender, surrender needs strength, great strength. If you surrender out of weakness, your surrender is meaningless, impotent. If you surrender out of strength, then your surrender has meaning, significance. At the sixth center, when will comes to its ultimate focusing, surrender is possible. Out of will is created surrender: out of man, God created woman.

At the sixth center… Now if you ask the brain surgeons, they will also agree with me – they say the brain is divided into two hemispheres: man and woman, the left and the right. The left brain is male and the right brain is female. The right brain is connected with the left hand; that's why the left hand is not appreciated – even condemned. The right hand is associated with the left brain – hence, right seems to be right and left seems to be wrong. It is a man-oriented world, male-dominated world. The right hand is the symbol of the male, the left hand is the symbol of the female. And your head is divided into two hemispheres.

A poet functions from a different part of his head than a logician. A poet is more feminine. It is not just a coincidence that if you look at great poets you will find great femininity, grace, beauty, a charm, a tremendous attraction, a charisma, feminine charisma. If you look at painters you will find them a little effeminate; their dress, their long hair, their way of walking, is more feminine.

I have heard...

In India, there was a very compassionate bodhisattva, but when Buddhism reached China, they could not believe that he could be a man: How is such compassion possible in a man? So they made statues of him as a woman. Those statues are called Kuan Yin, and they are still worshipped. The story is beautiful.

The Buddhist monks who carried Buddha's message to China tried to explain: "You are foolish. This is not a woman, but a man."

But the sculptors said: "We cannot do it. Our understanding is that such compassion is possible only in a woman, not a man." So they depicted a woman.

The story is of tremendous import. Buddha looks more like a woman than like a man – his face, his grace. The sixth center has been surrendered. Logic has been surrendered to love, argument has been surrendered to feeling; aggression has become reception. Conflict has turned into cooperation. Now there is no struggle between the part and the whole; the part is flowing with the whole, the part is in a let-go – the whole has possessed it.

That is the meaning of the Christian allegory that God

created man first, and then woman out of man. This is to pay tremendous respect to feminine qualities: they are higher than man, they come out of man, they flower out of man. And then, on the seventh day, God rested. What else can you do when you have come home? *Sahasrar* is the center of rest, absolute rest – you have arrived; now there is nowhere to go.

The lowest – *muladhar* – is the center of unrest, the highest is the center of rest, and between these two there are seven divisions. You can call them seven colors – yes, man is a rainbow. Or, you can call them seven notes of music. Eastern music divides sound into seven notes: *sa, re, ga, ma, pa, dha, ni* – these are the seven basic notes. And out of these seven basic notes all music is created – all symphony, all melody, all song, all dance.

Remember, seven is a very significant number.

And one more thing: to be more modern and contemporary, I would like to divide these seven centers in this way. The first I call *no-mind*. No-mind means the mind is fast asleep – *muladhar*. It is there, but so fast asleep that you cannot even detect it. In a rock, God is fast asleep. In man he has become a little alert – just a *little* alert, not very much. In a rock he is fast asleep, snoring. If you listen closely you will hear the snoring – God snoring. That's why rocks are so beautiful – so deeply silent, no turmoil, no anxiety, nowhere to go. This I call no-mind. I don't mean by no-mind that they have *no* mind; I simply mean the mind has not manifested yet. The mind is waiting in seed, the mind is getting ready to awake, the mind is preparing, the mind is resting. Sooner or later there will be morning and the rock will become a bird and will start flying, or will become a tree and will start blossoming.

The second state I call *unconscious mind*. In the trees, the mind is there – not like the rock, God has become a little different from the rock. Not conscious, unconscious. Trees feel – they cannot feel that they feel, but they feel. Listen to the difference. If you hit a tree she feels it, but she cannot feel that she feels it. That much awareness has not happened. Feeling has come in, the tree is sensitive. And now there are modern experiments proving it, that trees are tremendously sensitive.

This I call unconscious mind. Mind is there – almost like when one is asleep. In the morning one remembers that it was a beautiful night: "I slept deeply, the sleep was very profound." But you remember in the morning, not when the actual sleep is happening; you remember later on, retrospectively. Mind was there in sleep, but was not functioning at that moment; it only functions retrospectively, later on. In the morning you remember – a beautiful night, such a soothing and satiny night, such deep silence and such happiness – but you recognize it in the morning.

The third state is *subconscious* mind. Subconscious mind is in the birds, animals. It is like dreaming. In a dream you become a little more conscious than you are in your sleep. Let us say the rocks are in a coma; in the morning they will not even be able to remember how profound the sleep was – it is a coma. The trees are asleep; when they awake, they will remember. The birds and the animals are dreaming – they are very close to humanity. I call this the subconscious mind.

The fourth I call *conscious mind*. That's where man is. Not very conscious; just a flicker, just a small wave of consciousness – and that too happens only when you are in tremendous danger, otherwise not. If somebody suddenly comes and is ready to kill you with a dagger, you will become conscious. In that moment there will be tremendous awareness, intelligence, radiance. Thinking will stop. You will become a flame. Only in rare moments do you really become conscious; otherwise, you move almost like a somnambulist.

I have heard…

In 1959, two drunkards in the French town of Vienne opened what they thought was a door to the street. Actually it was the window of a room four stories up. With a gay song on their lips they marched out, arm in arm over the sill to the street below.

A beat policeman, hearing the thuds and rushing to help, was dumbfounded to watch them careering away, still singing and obviously in tip-top condition. "We missed our step," they explained.

They were not aware at all. Had they been aware, they might have died. They were not aware; they simply thought they had missed a step. Four stories!

And this is your situation too. Your whole life is almost that of a drunkard. You go on stumbling here and there, missing one step here, another step there. Your whole life is nothing but misery upon misery, stumbling, bumping into each other. You may call it love, but what it comes to is just bumping into each other. It creates misery.

Only consciousness can give ecstasy. Ecstasy is the shadow of consciousness. This is the fourth stage in which ordinarily human beings live and die. This is a sheer wastage. Rocks can be forgiven and trees can be forgiven and birds can be forgiven, but not man – because you have the first glimpse: now it is your responsibility to grow it, to make it more solid, to make it stronger. You cannot say to a rock: "You missed," but you can say to a man: "You missed."

Man is the only responsible animal – he can be asked, he will have to answer: that is the meaning of responsibility. One day or other, he will have to answer to God or to the center of this existence or to existence itself: "How did you miss? You were given the rudimentary beginning, you could have grown it. You were given the seed, you could have blossomed. Why did you miss?"

That's the anxiety of man, the agony, the trembling, the anguish – because man is the only animal in this world who can become ecstatic, who can achieve to conscious blissfulness, who can become *sat-chit-anand*: who can become truth, consciousness, being, who can become bliss, who can come to the ultimate.

The fifth I call the *sub-superconscious mind*. At the fourth stage – the conscious mind – your consciousness is just a very flickering thing, very momentary. It has no stability, comes and goes, and is beyond your power; you cannot recall it when it is needed. All religions exist between the conscious and the super-conscious mind. All techniques of yoga, all techniques as such, are nothing but to transform your consciousness into the super-consciousness. Gurdjieff calls it self-remembering. Kabir calls it Surati Yoga – *surati* also means remembering. Jesus says again and again: "Be aware! Be awake! Watch!" Buddha says: "Be alert." Krishnamurti goes on talking about awareness; for forty years he has been talking about only one thing, and that is awareness. One word is the whole message: that word is the bridge between conscious mind and superconscious mind.

When your consciousness has become a stable factor in you, an integrated factor in you, a crystallized factor in you, and you can depend on it.... Right now, you cannot depend on it. You are going along, very conscious, and somebody hits you – immediately the consciousness is gone; it is not dependable. Somebody says a simple word, somebody says to you, "Are you an idiot?" – and consciousness is gone. Just the word *idiot* and your eyes are bloodshot, and you are ready to be killed or to kill.

Even people who seem to be very, very alert and aware may be just alert and aware because they have escaped the situations. Their alertness is not real. You can go to the Himalayas, you can sit in a cave – nobody will come to call you an idiot. Who will bother to come to a Himalayan cave to call you an idiot? Of course you will not get angry. Your state of awareness in a Himalayan cave is not worth much because there is no test for it, no possibility to destroy it. Hence, Kabir says: "Be in the world. Don't be of the world, but be in the world, live in the world." Live in the ordinary situations where everything provokes you to be unconscious and everybody helps you to be conscious.

If you understand it, the world is a great device of God to make you more conscious. Your enemy is your friend, and the curses are blessings, and the misfortunes can be turned into fortunes. It depends only on one thing: if you know the key of awareness. Then you can turn everything into gold. When somebody insults you, that is the moment to keep alert. When your wife looks at somebody else and you feel hurt, that is the moment to keep alert. When you are feeling sad, gloomy, depressed, when you feel the whole world is against you, that is the moment to be alert. When you are surrounded by a dark night, that is the moment to keep your light burning. And all those situations will prove helpful – they are meant for it.

From the conscious mind to the superconscious mind is all yoga, meditation, prayer, awareness. Sub-superconscious mind is an integrated phenomenon, but you will still lose it sometimes. Not ordinarily when you are wakeful, but you may lose it when you go to sleep. Sub-superconscious mind will help you while you are wakeful, and sometimes even in dreams you may remember – but not in deep sleep. When Krishna says in the Gita, "The yogi is awake even when the whole world sleeps," he is indicating toward a higher state which I call the sixth – the *superconscious mind.* Then one remains alert even while asleep; deep asleep, but awareness remains there. This is the sixth. And out of this sixth, the seventh grows spontaneously – you have not to do anything for it.

That seventh I again call *no-mind*, to make the circle complete. The first is the no-mind of a rock and the last is the no-mind of a God. To show this unity, we have sculptured Gods in stone. To show this unity, this circle complete, we have made stone statues of God to show that stone is the first and God is the last and both meet somewhere. Again, no-mind – call it soul, God, enlightenment, nirvana, salvation, or whatsoever you choose to call it.

These are the seven stages. And this is the rainbow a man is.

One thing more, and that is: not a single color has to be denied. All the colors have to be absorbed in the rainbow, and all the notes of music, all the seven notes of music, have to become part of the melody, and all these seven chakras from *muladhar* to *sahasrar* have to become a unity. It is not that you have to deny some chakras, because that denied chakra will never allow you to become whole – and one who is not whole can never be holy. They all have to form a hierarchy, a unity; they all have to belong to one center.

A real man of religion lives the whole rainbow, from the rock to God – from no-mind on this end to the no-mind on the other end. He is the whole spectrum. He lives life totally. Nothing is denied, everything is used. Nothing is denied at all; if something feels like a jarring note, that simply means you have not yet been able to utilize it. It can be used, the poison can become medicinal – you have to know how to transform it. And sometimes the nectar can be poisonous if you don't know how to use it.

If you know how to use anger, you will see anger gives you a sharpness of being – just as if somebody has sharpened a sword. Anger rightly used gives you a sharpness, a radiance, a tremendous vitality. Sex rightly used makes you so full of love that you can go on sharing with all and sundry and it is never exhausted. Sex rightly used gives a rebirth to yourself. Ordinarily, it reproduces children; extraordinarily, it reproduces your innermost being.

Let me tell you that whatever you have, all has to be used – nothing is useless. Never throw anything away, otherwise you will repent one day. All has to be used. Just become more insightful, more mindful; become more aware, and start looking into things of your inner being and how to bring them to a higher harmony – that's all. Right now you are a crowd. Right now you are not an individual. You are not a rainbow – all the colors are falling in separate dimensions, moving away from each other; they don't have a center. Right now you are a noise, not music – but remember, all the notes are present in the noise. Rearranged, arranged in a better, aesthetic, artistic way, they will become beautiful music. All that is needed is a deep aesthetic look into your being.

CHAPTER 3

Understanding the Chakras and Kundalini

No theoretical knowledge ever helps and no anatomical visualization of kundalini is really meaningful for meditation. When I say this, I do not mean that there is nothing like kundalini or chakras. Kundalini is there, the chakras are there, but no knowledge helps in any way. Rather, it can hinder. It can become a barrier for so many reasons.

One reason is that any knowledge about kundalini or about esoteric paths of bioenergy – the inner paths of elan vital – is generalized. It differs from individual to individual; the root is not going to be the same. With *A* it will be one thing, with *B* it will be different, with *C* it will be different. Your inner life has an individuality, so when you acquire something through theoretical knowledge it is not going to help – it may hinder – because it is not about you. It cannot be about you. You will only know about yourself when you go within.

There are chakras, but the number differs with each individual. One may have seven, one may have nine; one may have more, one may have less. That is the reason why so many different traditions have developed. Buddhists talk of nine chakras, Hindus talk of seven, Tibetans talk of four – and they are all right!

The root of kundalini, the passage through which kundalini passes, is also different with each individual. The more you go in, the more individual you are. For instance, your face is the most individual part of your body, and in the face the eyes are even more individual. The face is more alive than any other part of the body; that is why it takes on an individuality. You may not have noticed that with a particular age – particularly with sexual maturity – your face begins to assume a shape that will continue, more or less, for the whole life. Before sexual maturity the face changes much, but with sexual maturity your individuality is fixed and given a pattern, and now the face will be more or less the same.

The eyes are even more alive than the face, and they are so individual that they change every moment. Unless one attains enlightenment, the eyes are never fixed. Enlightenment is another kind of maturity.

With sexual maturity the face becomes fixed, but there is another maturity where the eyes become fixed. You cannot see any change in Buddha's eyes: his body will grow old, he will die, but his eyes will continue to be the same. That has been one of the indications. When someone attains nirvana, the eyes are the only door by which outsiders can know whether the man has really attained it. Now the eyes never change. Everything changes, but the eyes remain the same. Eyes are expressive of the inner world.

But kundalini is still deeper.

No theoretical knowledge is helpful. When you have some theoretical knowledge, you begin to impose it on yourself. You begin to visualize things to be the way you have been taught, but they may not correspond to your individual situation. Then much confusion is created.

One has to feel the chakras, not know *about* them. You have to feel; you have to send feelers inside yourself. Only when you feel your chakras, and your kundalini and its passage, is it helpful; otherwise, it is not helpful. In fact, knowledge has been very destructive as far as the inner world is concerned. The more knowledge gained, the less the possibility of feeling the real, the authentic, things.

You begin to impose what you know upon yourself. If someone says, "Here is the chakra, here is the center," then you begin to visualize your chakra at that spot; and it may not be there at all. Then you will create imaginary chakras. You can create; the mind has the capacity. You can create imaginary chakras, and then, because of your imagination, a flow will begin that will not be kundalini but will be simple imagination – a completely illusory, dreamlike phenomenon.

Once you can visualize centers and can create an imaginary kundalini, then you can create everything. Then imaginary experiences will follow, and you will develop a very false world inside you. The world that is without is illusory, but not as illusory as the one you can create inside.

All that is within is not necessarily real or true, because imagination is also within, dreams are also within. The mind has a faculty – a very powerful faculty – to dream, to create illusions, to project. That is why it is good to proceed in meditation completely unaware of kundalini, of the chakras. If you stumble upon them, then it is good. You may come to feel something; only then, ask. You may begin to feel a chakra working, but let the feeling come first. You may feel energy rising up, but let the feeling come first. Do not imagine, do not think about it, do not make any intellectual effort to understand beforehand; no pre-notion is needed. Not only is it not needed, but it is positively harmful.

And another thing: kundalini and the chakras do not belong to your anatomy, to your physiology. The chakras and kundalini belong to your subtle body, to your *sukshma sharira*, not to this body, the gross body. Of course, there are corresponding spots. The chakras are part of your *sukshma sharira*, but your physiology and anatomy have spots that correspond to them. If you feel an inner chakra, only then can you feel the corresponding spot; otherwise you can dissect the whole body, but nothing like chakras will be found.

All the talk and all the so-called evidence and all the scientific claims that your gross body has something like kundalini and chakras is nonsense, absolute nonsense. There are corresponding spots, but those spots can only be felt when you feel the real chakras. With the dissection of your gross body, nothing can be found; there is nothing. So the question is not of anatomy.

One more thing: it is not necessary to pass through the chakras. It is not necessary; one can just bypass them. It is also not necessary that you will feel kundalini before enlightenment. The phenomenon is very different from what you may think. Kundalini is not felt because it is rising; kundalini is only felt if you do not have a very clear passage. If the passage is completely clear-cut, then the energy flows but you cannot feel it.

You feel it when there is something there that resists the flow. If the energy flows upward and you have blocks in the passage, only then do you feel it. So the person who feels more kundalini is really blocked: there are many blocks in the passage, so the kundalini cannot flow.

When there is resistance, then the kundalini is felt. You cannot feel energy directly unless there is resistance. If I move my hand and there is no resistance, the movement will not be felt. The movement is felt because the air resists, but it is not felt as much as when a stone resists; then I will feel the movement more. And in a vacuum I will not feel the movement at all – so it is relative.

Buddha never talked about kundalini. It is not that there was no kundalini in his body, but the passage was so clear that there was no resistance. Thus, he never felt it. Mahavira never talked about kundalini. Because of this, a very false notion was created, and then Jainas, who followed Mahavira, thought that kundalini was all nonsense, that there was nothing like it. Thus, because Mahavira himself did not feel kundalini, twenty-five centuries of Jaina tradition has continued to deny it, claiming it does not exist. But Mahavira's reason for not talking about it was very different. Because there were no blocks in his body, he never felt it.

So it is not necessary for you to feel kundalini. You may not feel it at all. And if you do not feel kundalini, then you will bypass the chakras, because the working of the chakras is needed only to break the blocks. Otherwise, they are not needed.

When there is a block, and the kundalini is blocked, then the nearby chakra begins to move because of the blocked kundalini. It becomes dynamic. The chakra begins to move because of the blocked kundalini and it moves so fast that, because of the movement, a particular energy is created which breaks the block.

If the passage is clear, no chakra is needed and you will never feel anything. Really, the existence of chakras is just to help you. If kundalini is blocked, then the help is just nearby. Some chakra will take the energy that is being blocked. If the energy cannot move further it will fall back. Before it falls back, the chakra will absorb the energy completely, and the kundalini will move in the chakra. Through movement the energy becomes more vital, it becomes more alive, and when it again comes to the block it can break it. So it is just an arrangement, a help.

If kundalini moves and there are no blocks, then you will never feel any of the chakras. That is why someone may feel nine chakras, someone else may feel ten chakras, and someone else may feel only three or four, or one, or none. It depends. In actual fact, there are infinite chakras and at every movement, every step of the kundalini, a chakra is by the side to help. If the help is needed, it can be given.

That is why I insist that a theoretical acquaintance is not helpful. And meditation as such is not really concerned with kundalini at all. If kundalini comes, that is another thing – but meditation has nothing to do with it. Meditation can be explained without even mentioning kundalini; there is no need. And by mentioning kundalini it creates even more conflicts to explaining meditation. Meditation can be explained directly; you need not bother about chakras, you begin with meditation. If the passage is blocked you may come to feel kundalini, and chakras will be there, but that is completely nonvoluntary. You must remember that it is nonvoluntary; your volition is not needed at all.

The deeper the path, the more nonvoluntary. I can move my hand – this is a voluntary path – but I cannot move my blood. I can try. Years and years of training can make a person capable of making the blood circulation voluntary – hatha yoga can do that; it has been done, it is not impossible, but it is futile. Thirty years of training just to control the movement of the blood is mean-ingless and stupid because with the control comes nothing. The blood circulation is nonvoluntary; your will is not needed. You take in food and the moment it goes in, your will is not needed: the body machinery, the body mechanism, has taken over, and it goes on doing whatever is needed. Your sleep is not voluntary, your birth is not voluntary, your death is not voluntary. These are nonvoluntary mechanisms.

Kundalini is still deeper, deeper than your death, deeper than your birth, deeper than your blood, because kundalini is a circulation of your second body. Blood is the circulation of your physiological body; kundalini is the circulation of your *etheric* body. It is absolutely nonvoluntary; even a hatha yogi cannot do anything with it voluntarily.

One has to go into meditation, then the energy begins to move. The part that is to be done by you is meditation. If you are deeply in in it, then the inner energy begins to move upward, and you will feel the change of flow. It will be felt in so many ways: the change can even be known physiologically.

For example, ordinarily, biologically, it is a sign of good

health for your feet to be warm and your head to be cool. Biologically it is a healthy sign. When the reverse occurs – the feet become cool and the head becomes warm – a person is ill. But the same thing happens when the kundalini flows upward: the feet become cool.

Really, the warmth in the feet is nothing but sex energy flowing downward. The moment the vital energy, the kundalini, begins to flow upward, sex energy follows. It begins to flow upward: the feet become cool and the head becomes warm. Biologically it is better for the feet to be warmer than the head, but spiritually it is healthier for the feet to be cooler because this is a sign that the energy is flowing upward.

Many diseases may begin to occur once the energy begins to flow upward, because biologically you have disturbed the whole organism. Buddha died very ill, Mahavira died very ill, Raman Maharshi died with cancer; Ramakrishna died with cancer. And the reason is that the whole biological system is disturbed. Many other reasons are given, but they are nonsense.

Jainas have created many stories because they could not conceive that Mahavira could have been ill. For me, the contrary is the case: I cannot conceive how he could have been completely healthy. He couldn't be, because this was going to be his last birth, and the whole biological system had to break down. A system that had been continuous for millennia had to break down. He could not be healthy; in the end he had to be very ill. And he was! But it was very difficult for his followers to conceive that Mahavira was ill.

There was only one explanation for illness in those days. If you were suffering from a particular disease, it meant your karmas your past deeds, had been bad. If Mahavira was suffering from a disease, then it would have meant that he was still under his karmic influence. This could not be so, so an ingenious story was invented: that Goshalak, a competitor of Mahavira, was using evil forces against him. But this was not the case at all.

The biological, natural flow is downward; the spiritual flow is upward. And the whole organism is meant for a downward flow.

You may begin to feel many changes in the body, but the first changes will come in the subtle body. Meditation is just the means to create a bridge from the gross to the subtle. When I say meditation, I mean only that: if you can jump out of your gross body – that is what is meant by meditation. But to take this jump you will need the help of your gross body; you will have to use it as a stepping-stone.

From any extreme point, you can take the jump. Fasting has been used to take one to an extreme. With long, continuous fasting, you come to the verge. The human body can ordinarily sustain a ninety-day fast, but then, the moment the body is completely exhausted, the moment the reservoir that has been accumulated for emergencies has been depleted – at that moment, one of two things is possible. If you do nothing, death may occur, but if you use this moment for meditation, the jump may occur.

If you do not do anything, if you just go on fasting, death may occur. Then it will be suicide. Mahavira, who experimented more deeply with fasting than anyone else in the whole history of human evolution, is the only man who allowed his followers a spiritual suicide. He called it *santhara*: that on-the-verge point when both things are possible. In a single moment, you may either die or you can jump. If you use a technique, you can jump; then, Mahavira says, it is not suicide, but a very great spiritual explosion. Mahavira was the only man – the only one – who has said that if you have the courage, even suicide can be used for your spiritual progress.

From any point on the verge, the jump is possible. Sufis have used dancing. A moment comes in dancing when you begin to feel unearthly. With a real Sufi dancer, even the audience begins to feel unearthly. Through body movements, rhythmic movements, the dancer soon begins to feel that he is different from the body, separate from the body. One has to begin the movement but soon a nonvoluntary mechanism of the body takes over.

You begin, but if the end is also yours then the dancing was just ordinary dancing. But if you begin and by the end you feel as if somewhere in between the dancing was taken over by a nonvoluntary mechanism, then it has become a dervish dance. You move so fast that the body shakes and becomes nonvoluntary.

That is the point where you can go crazy or you can jump. You may go mad, because a nonvoluntary mechanism has taken over your body movement. It is beyond your control: you cannot do anything. You may just go mad and never be able to come back again from this nonvoluntary movement. This is the point where there is either madness or, if you know the technique to jump, meditation.

That is why Sufis have always been known as mad people. They have been known as mad. Ordinarily, they are mad. There is also a sect in Bengal that is just like the Sufis: Baul fakirs. They move from village to village dancing and singing. The very word *baul* means *bawla*, mad. They are people who are mad.

Madness happens many times, but if you know the technique, then meditation can happen. It always happens on the verge; that is why mystics have always used the term "the sword's edge." Either madness may happen or meditation may happen, and every method uses your body as a sword's edge from which either one or the other is possible.

Then what is the technique to jump into meditation? I have talked about two: fasting and dancing. All techniques of meditation are to push you to the verge where you can take the jump, but the jump itself can be taken only through a very simple, very non-methodical method.

If you can be aware at the very moment when fasting has led you to the precipice of death, if you can be aware at the moment when death is going to set in, if you can be aware, then there is no death. And not only is there no death this time, then there is no death forever. You have jumped! When the moment is so intense that you know in one second it will be beyond you, when you know that should a second be lost you will not be able to come back again, be aware – and then jump. Awareness is the method. And because awareness is the method, Zen people say that there is no method. Awareness is not a method at all. That is why Krishnamurti will go on saying that there is no method.

Of course, awareness is not really a method at all; but I still call it a method because if you cannot be aware, then at the exact moment that the jump is possible, you will be lost. So if someone says, "Only awareness will do," that may be true for one out of ten thousand people, but that one will be one who has come to the point where either madness is possible or death is possible. He has come to that point anyway.

And with the others, the majority of people, just talking about awareness will not do. First, they must be trained. To be aware in ordinary situations will not do. And you cannot be aware in ordinary situations. The mind's stupidity has such a long history – the lethargy of it, the laziness of it, the unconsciousness of it, has been going on for so long, that just by hearing Krishnamurti or me or anyone else you can never hope to be aware. And it will be difficult to be aware of those same things that you have done without awareness so many times.

You have come to your office completely unaware that you have been moving: you have turned, you have walked, you have opened the door. For your whole life you have been doing it. Now it has become a nonvoluntary mechanism; it has been removed from your consciousness completely.

Then Krishnamurti says, "Be aware when you are walking." But you have been walking without ever being aware. The habit has set in so deeply, it has become a part of the bones and blood; now it is very difficult.

You can only be aware in emergencies, in sudden emergencies. Someone puts a gun to your chest: you can be aware because it is a situation that you have never practiced. But if you are familiar with the situation, you will not be aware at all.

Fasting is to create an emergency, and such an emergency as you have never known. So one who has been practicing fasting may not be helped through it; he will need longer periods to fast. Or, if you have never danced, you can be helped easily through dancing; but if you are an expert dancer, Sufi dervish dancing will not do. It will not do at all because you are so perfect, so efficient, and efficiency means that the thing is now being done by the nonvoluntary part of the mind. Efficiency always means that.

That is why one hundred and twelve methods of meditation have been developed. One may not do for you; another may. And the one which will be most helpful is the one which is completely unknown to you. If you have never been trained in a particular method at all, then an emergency is created very soon. And in that emergency, be aware!

So be concerned with meditation and not with kundalini. And when you are aware, things will begin to happen in you. For the first time you will become aware of an inner world that is greater, vaster, more extensive than the universe; energies unknown, completely unknown, will begin to flow in you. Phenomena never heard of, never imagined, or dreamed of, will begin to happen. But with each person they differ, so it is good not to talk about them.

CHAPTER 4

Seven Subtle Bodies and
the Energy of Breath

Prana is energy – the living energy in us, the life in us. This life manifests itself, as far as the physical body is concerned, as the incoming and the outgoing breath. These are two opposite things; we take them as one. We say "breathing" – but breathing has two polarities: the incoming breath and the outgoing breath. Every energy has polarities, every energy exists in two opposite poles. It cannot exist otherwise. The opposite poles, with their tension and harmony, create energy – just like magnetic poles.

The incoming breath is quite contrary to the outgoing, and the outgoing is quite contrary to the incoming. In a single moment, the incoming is just like birth and the outgoing is just like death. In a single moment both things are happening: when you take breath in, you are born; when you throw breath out, you die. In a single moment there is birth and death. This polarity is life energy coming up, going down.

In the physical body, life energy takes this manifestation. Life energy is born, and after seventy years it dies. That too is a greater manifestation of the same phenomenon: the incoming breath and the outgoing breath – the day and the night.

In all of the seven bodies – the physical, the *etheric*, the astral, the mental, the spiritual, the cosmic, and the nirvanic, there will be a corresponding incoming and outgoing phenomenon.

As far as the mental body is concerned, thought coming in and thought going out is the same kind of phenomenon as breath coming in and breath going out. Every moment a thought comes in your mind and a thought goes out. Thought itself is energy. In the mental body, the energy manifests as the coming of thought and the going of thought; in the physical body, it manifests as breath coming and breath going. That is why you can change your thinking with breathing. There is a correspondence.

If you stop your breath from coming in, thought will be stopped from coming in. Stop your breath in your physical body and in the mental body thought will stop. And as the physical body becomes uneasy, your mental body will become uneasy. The physical body will long to breathe in; the mental body will long to take in thought.

Just as breath is taken in from the outside and the air exists outside you, likewise an ocean of thought exists outside you. Thought comes in, and thought goes out. Your breath can become my breath at another moment and your thought can become my thought. Every time you throw your breath out, you are likewise throwing your thought out. Just as air exists, so thought exists; just as air can be contaminated, so thought can be contaminated; just as air can be impure, so thought can be impure.

The breath itself is not *prana*. *Prana* means the vital energy that manifests itself by these polarities of coming in and going out. The energy that takes the breath in is *prana*, not the breath itself. The energy that takes breath in, which asserts it, the energy that is taking the breath in and throwing it out, is *prana*.

The energy that takes thought in and throws thought out, that energy too is *prana*. In all of the seven bodies, this process exists. I am only talking now of the physical and the mental, because these two are known to us; we can understand them easily. But in every layer of your being the same thing exists.

Your second body, the *etheric* body, has its own incoming and outgoing process. You will feel this process in each of the seven bodies, but you will feel it to be just like the incoming breath and outgoing breath, because you are only acquainted with your physical body and its *prana*. Then you will always misunderstand.

Whenever any feeling comes to you of another body or its *prana*, you will first understand it as the coming in and the going out of breath, because this is the only experience you know. You have only known this manifestation of *prana*, of vital energy. But on the etheric plane there is neither breath nor thought, but influence – simply influence coming in and going out.

You come into contact with somebody without having known him before. He has not even talked with you, but something about him comes in. You have either taken him in or thrown him out. There is a subtle influence: you may call it love or you may call it hatred – the attractive or the repulsive.

When you are repulsed or attracted, it is your second body. And every moment the process is going on; it never stops. You are always taking influences in and then throwing them out. The other pole will always be there. If you have loved someone, then in a certain moment you will be repulsed. If you have loved someone the breath has been taken in: now it will be thrown out and you will be repulsed. So every moment of love will be followed by a moment of repulsion.

The vital energy exists in polarities. It never exists at one pole. It cannot! And whenever you try to make it do so, you try the impossible.

You cannot love someone without hating him at some time. The hatred will be there because the vital force cannot exist at a single pole. It exists at opposite polarities, so a friend is bound to be an enemy – and this will go on. This coming in and going out will happen up to the seventh body. No body can exist without this process – this coming in and going out. It cannot, just as the physical body cannot exist without the incoming and outgoing breath.

As far as the physical body is concerned, we never take these two things as opposites, so we are not disturbed about it. Life makes no distinction between the incoming breath and the outgoing breath. There is no moral distinction. There is nothing to be chosen; both are the same. The phenomenon is natural.

But as far as the second body is concerned, hatred must not be there and love must be there. Then you have begun to choose. You have begun to choose, and this choice will create disturbances. That is why the physical body is ordinarily more healthy than the second, the etheric, body. The etheric body is always in conflict because moral choosing has made a hell out of it.

When love comes to you, you feel well-being, but when hatred comes to you, you feel diseased. But it is bound to come – so a person who knows, a person who has understood the polarities, is not disappointed when it comes. A person who has known the polarities is at ease, at equilibrium. He knows it is bound to happen, so he neither tries to love when he is not loving nor does he create any hatred. Things come and go: he is not attracted to the incoming nor repulsed by the outgoing. He is just a witness. He says, "It is just like breath coming in and breath going out."

The Buddhist meditation method of Anapanasati Yoga is concerned with this. It says to just be a witness to your incoming and outgoing breath. Just be a witness, and begin from the physical body. The other six bodies are not talked about in Anapanasati because they will come by themselves, by and by.

The more you become acquainted with this polarity – with this dying and living simultaneously, with this simultaneous birth and death – the more you will become aware of the second body. Toward hatred, then, Buddha says, have *upeksha*. Be indifferent.

Whether it is hatred or it is love, be indifferent. And do not be attached to anyone because if you are attached, what will happen to the other pole? Then you will be at a "dis-ease." Disease will be there; you will not be at ease.

Buddha says, "The coming of the beloved one is welcomed, but the going of the beloved one is wept over. The meeting with the one who is repulsive is a misery, and the departing of a repulsive one is bliss. But if you go on dividing yourself into these polarities, you will be in hell, living in a hell."

If you just become a witness to these polarities, then you say, "This is a natural phenomenon. It is natural to the body concerned" – that is, one of the seven bodies. "The body exists because of this; otherwise, it cannot exist." And the moment you become aware of it, you transcend the body. If you transcend your first body, then you become aware of the second. If you transcend your second body, then you become aware of the third.

Witnessing is always beyond life and death. The breath coming in and the breath going out are two things, and if you become a witness, then you are neither. Then a third force has come into being. Now you are not the manifestations of *prana* in the physical body: now you *are* the *prana*, the witness. Now you see that life manifests on the physical level because of this polarity, and if this polarity stops, the physical body will not be there, it cannot exist. It needs tension to exist – this constant tension of coming and going, this constant tension of birth and death. It exists because of this. Every moment it moves between the two poles; otherwise, it would not exist.

In the second body, "love and hate" is the basic polarity. It is manifested in so many ways. The basic polarity is this liking and disliking, and every moment your liking becomes disliking and your disliking becomes liking – every moment! But you never see it. When your liking becomes disliking, if you suppress your disliking and continue fooling yourself that you will go on liking the same things always, you are only doubly fooling yourself. And if you dislike something, you go on disliking it, never allowing yourself to see the moments when you have liked it. We suppress our love for our enemies, and we suppress our hatred for our friends. We are suppressing. We allow only one movement, only one pole, but because it comes back again, we are at ease. It returns, so we are at ease. But it is discontinuous; it is never continuous. It never can be.

The vital force manifests itself as like and dislike in the second body. But it is just like breath: there is no difference. Influence is the medium here; air is the medium in the physical body. The second body lives in an atmosphere of influences. It is not simply that someone comes in contact with you and you begin to like him. Even if no one comes in and you are alone in the room, you will be liking–disliking, liking–disliking. It will make no difference: the liking and disliking will go on continuously alternating.

It is through this polarity that the etheric body exists; it is its breath. If you become a witness to it, then you can just laugh. Then there is no enemy and no friend. Then you know it is just a natural phenomenon.

If you become aware and become a witness to the second body – to the liking and disliking – then you can know the third body. The third is the astral body. Just like the "influences" of the etheric body, the astral body has "magnetic forces." Its magnetism is its breath. One moment you are powerful and the next moment you are powerless; one moment you are hopeful and the next moment you are hopeless; one moment you are confident and the next moment you lose all your confidence. It is a coming in of magnetism to you and a going out of magnetism from you. There are moments when you can defy even God, and there are moments when you fear even a shadow.

When the magnetic force is in you, when it is coming into you, you are great; when it has gone from you, you are just a nobody. And this is changing back and forth, just like day and night; the circle revolves, the wheel revolves. So even a person like Napoleon had his impotent moments and even a very cowardly person has his moments of bravery.

In judo there is a technique to know when a person is powerless. That is the moment to attack him. When he is powerful you are bound to be defeated, so you have to know the moment when his magnetic power is going out and attack him then, and you should incite him to attack you when your magnetic force is coming in.

This coming in and going out of the magnetic force corresponds to your breathing. That is why, when you have to do something difficult, you will hold your breath in. For example, if you are to lift a heavy stone, you cannot pick it up when the breath is going out. You cannot do it! But when the breath is coming in, or when the breath is held in, you can do it. Your breath corresponds to what is happening in the third body. So when the breath is going out – unless the person has been trained to fool you – that is the moment when his magnetic force is going out; that is the moment to attack. And this is the secret of judo. Even a stronger person than you can be defeated if you know the secret of when he is fearful and powerless. When the magnetic force is out of him, he is bound to be powerless.

The third body lives in a magnetic sphere, just like air. There are magnetic forces all around: you are breathing them in and breathing them out. But if you become aware of this magnetic force that is coming and going, then you are neither powerful nor powerless. You transcend both.

Then there is the fourth body, the mental body: thought pulling in and thought pulling out. But this "thought coming in" and "thought going out" has parallels, too. When thought comes to you while you breathe in, only in those moments is original thinking born. When you breathe out, those are moments of impotency; no original thought can be born in those moments. In moments when some original thought is there, the breathing will even stop. When an original thought is born, then the breath stops. It is only a corresponding phenomenon.

In the outgoing thought, nothing is born. It is simply dead. But if you become aware of thoughts coming in and thoughts going out, then you can know the fifth body.

Up to the fourth body, things are not difficult to understand because we have some experience which can become the basis to understand them. Beyond the fourth, things become very strange – but still, something can be understood. And when you transcend the fourth body you will understand it more.

In the fifth body – how to say it? The atmosphere for the fifth body is life – just as thought, as breath, as magnetic force, as love and hatred, are atmospheres for the lower bodies.

For the fifth body, life itself is the atmosphere. So in the fifth, the coming in is a moment of life, and the going out is a moment of death. With the fifth, you become aware that life is not something that is in you. It comes into you and goes out from you. Life itself is not in you; it simply comes in and goes out just like breath.

That is why breath and *prana* became synonymous – because of the fifth body. In the fifth body, the word *prana* is meaningful. It is life that is coming and life that is going. And that is why the fear of death is constantly following us. You are always aware that death is nearby, waiting at the corner. It is always there, waiting. This feeling of death always waiting for you – this feeling of insecurity, of death, of darkness – is concerned with the fifth body. It is a very dark feeling, very vague, because you are not completely aware of it.

When you come to the fifth body and become aware of it, then you know that life and death both are just breaths to the fifth body – coming in and going out. And when you become aware of this, you know that you cannot die because death is not an inherent phenomenon; nor is life. Both life and death are outward phenomena happening to you. You never have been alive, you never have been dead; you are something that completely transcends both. But this feeling of transcendence can only come when you become aware of the life force and the death force in the fifth body.

Freud said somewhere that he somehow had a glimpse of this. He was not an adept in yoga, otherwise he would have understood it. He called it "the will to die," and he said every man sometimes is longing for life and sometimes is longing for death. There are two opposing wills in men: a will to live and a will to die. To the Western mind it was absolutely absurd: how could these contradictory wills exist in one person? But Freud said that because suicide is possible, there must be a will to die.

No animal can commit suicide, because no animal can become aware of the fifth body. Animals cannot commit suicide because they cannot become aware, they cannot know, that they are alive. To commit suicide, one thing is necessary: to be aware of life – and they are not aware of life. But another thing is also necessary: to commit suicide you must also be unaware of death.

Animals cannot commit suicide because animals are not aware of life, but we can commit suicide because we are aware of life but not aware of death. If one becomes aware of death, then one cannot commit suicide. A buddha cannot commit suicide because it is unnecessary; it is nonsense. He knows that you cannot really kill yourself, you can only pretend to. Suicide is just a pose because really you are neither alive nor dead.

Death is on the fifth plane, in the fifth body. It is a going out of a particular energy and a coming in of a particular energy. You are the one in which this coming and going happens. If you become identified with the first, you can commit the second. If you become identified with living, and if life becomes impossible, you can say, "I will commit suicide." This is the other aspect of your fifth body asserting itself. There is not a single human being who has not thought at some time to commit suicide – because death is the other side of life. This other side can become either suicide or murder: it can become either.

If you are obsessed with life, if you are so attached to it that you want to deny death completely, you can kill another. By killing another you satisfy your death wish: the will to die. By this trick you satisfy it, and you think that now you will not have to die because someone else has died.

All those who have committed great murders – Hitler, Mussolini – are still very much afraid of death. They are always in fear of death, so they project this death on others. The person who can kill someone else feels that he is more powerful than death: he can kill others. In a magical way, with a magical formula, he thinks that because he can kill he transcends death, that a thing he can do to others cannot be done to him. This is a projection of death, but it can come back to you. If you kill so many people that in the end you commit suicide, it is the projection coming back to you.

In the fifth body, with life and death coming to you – with life coming and going – one cannot be attached to anyone. If you are attached, you are not accepting the polarity in its totality, and you will become ill.

Up to the fourth body it was not so difficult, but to conceive of death and to accept it as another aspect of life is the most difficult act. To conceive of life and death as parallel – as just the same, as two aspects of one thing – is the most difficult act. But in the fifth, this is the polarity. This is *pranic* existence in the fifth.

With the sixth body, things become even more difficult because the sixth is no longer life. For the sixth body – what to say? After the fifth, the "I" drops, the ego drops. Then there is no ego; you become one with the all. Now it is not your "anything" that comes in and goes out because the ego is not. Everything becomes cosmic and because it becomes cosmic, the polarity takes the form of creation and destruction – *srishti* and *pralaya*. That is why it becomes more difficult with the sixth: the atmosphere is "the creative force and the destructive force." In Hindu mythology they call these forces Brahma and Shiva.

Brahma is the deity of creation, Vishnu is the deity of maintenance, and Shiva is the deity of the great death – of destruction or dissolution, where everything goes back to its original source. The sixth body is in that vast sphere of creativity and destructivity: the force of Brahma and the force of Shiva.

Every moment the creation comes to you, and every moment everything goes into dissolution. So when a yogi says, "I have seen the creation, and I have seen the *pralaya*, the end; I have seen the coming of the world into being and I have seen the returning of the world into nonbeing," he is talking about the sixth body. The ego is not there: everything that is coming in and going out is you. You become one with it.

A star is being born: it is your birth that is coming. And the star is going out: that is your going out. So they say in Hindu mythology that one creation is one breath of Brahma – only one breath! It is the cosmic force breathing. When he, Brahma, breathes in, the creation comes into existence: a star is born, stars come out of chaos – everything comes into existence. And when his breath goes out, everything goes out, everything ceases: a star dies – existence moves into nonexistence.

That is why I am saying that in the sixth body it is very difficult. The sixth is not egocentric; it becomes cosmic. And in the sixth body, everything about creation is known – everything that all of the religions of the world talk about. When one talks about creation, he is talking about the sixth body and the knowledge concerned with it. And when one is talking of the great flood, the end, one is talking about the sixth body.

With the great flood of Judeo-Christian or Babylonian mythology, or Syrian mythology, or with the *pralaya* of the Hindus, there is one out breath – that of the sixth body. This is a cosmic experience, not an individual one. This is a cosmic experience; you are not there!

The person who is in the sixth body – who has reached the

sixth body – will see everything that is dying as his own death. A Mahavira cannot kill an ant, not because of any principle of nonviolence, but because it is his death. Everything that dies is his death.

When you become aware of this, of the creation and the destruction – of things coming into existence every moment and things going out of existence every moment – the awareness is of the sixth body. Whenever a thing is going out of existence, something else is coming in: a sun is dying, another is being born somewhere else; this earth will die, another earth will come.

We become attached even in the sixth body. "Humanity must not die!" – but everything that is born must die, even humanity must die. Hydrogen bombs will be created to destroy it. And the moment we create hydrogen bombs, the very next moment we create a longing to go to another planet, because the bomb means that the earth is near its death. Before this earth dies, life will begin to evolve somewhere else.

The sixth body is the feeling of cosmic creation and destruction – creation–destruction; the breath coming in, the breath going out. That is why "Brahma's breath" is used. Brahma is a sixth-body personality; you become Brahma in the sixth body. Really, you become aware of both Brahma and Shiva, the two polarities. And Vishnu is beyond the polarity. They form the trimurti, the trinity: Brahma, Vishnu, and Mahesh – or Shiva.

This trinity is the trinity of witnessing. If you become aware of Brahma and Shiva, the creator and the destroyer – if you become aware of those two, then you know the third, which is Vishnu. Vishnu is your reality in the sixth body. That is why Vishnu became the most prominent of the three. Brahma is remembered, but although he is the god of creation, he is worshipped in perhaps only one or two temples. He must be worshipped, but he is not really worshipped.

Shiva is worshipped even more than Vishnu because we fear death. The worship of him comes out of our fear of death. But hardly anyone worships Brahma, the god of creation, because there is nothing to be fearful of; you are already created, so you are not concerned with Brahma. That is why not a single great temple is dedicated to him. He is the creator, so every temple should be dedicated to him, but it is not.

Shiva has the greatest number of worshippers. He is everywhere because so many temples were made as a dedication to him. Just a stone is enough to symbolize him; otherwise it would have been impossible to create so many idols of him. So just a stone is enough. Just put a stone somewhere and Shiva is there. Because the mind is so fearful of death, you cannot escape from Shiva; he must be worshipped – and he has been worshipped.

But Vishnu is the more substantial divinity. That is why Rama is an incarnation of Vishnu, Krishna is an incarnation of Vishnu, every *avatar* – divine incarnation – is an incarnation of Vishnu. And even Brahma and Shiva worship Vishnu. Brahma may be the creator, but he creates for Vishnu; Shiva may be the destroyer, but he destroys for Vishnu. These are the two breaths of Vishnu, the incoming and the outgoing: Brahma is the incoming breath and Shiva is the outgoing one. And Vishnu is the reality in the sixth body.

In the seventh body, things become even more difficult. Buddha called the seventh body the *nirvana kaya*, the body of enlightenment, because the truth, the absolute, is in the seventh body. The seventh body is the last body, so there is not even creation and destruction but, rather, being and nonbeing. In the seventh, creation is always of something else, it is not of you. Creation will be of something else and destruction will be of something else, not of you, while being is of you, and nonbeing is of you.

In the seventh body, being and nonbeing – existence and nonexistence – are the two breaths. One should not be identified with either. All religions are started by those who have reached the seventh body; and at the end language can be stretched, at the most, to two words: being and nonbeing. Buddha speaks the language of nonbeing, of the outgoing breath, so he says, "Nothingness is the reality"; while Shankara speaks the language of being and says that *brahman* is the ultimate reality. Shankara uses positive terms because he chooses the incoming breath, and Buddha uses negative terms because he chooses the outgoing breath. But these are the only choices as far as language is concerned.

The third choice is the reality, which cannot be said. At the most we can say "absolute being" or "absolute nonbeing." This much can be said, because the seventh body is beyond this. Transcendence is still possible.

I can say something about this room if I go out. If I transcend this room and reach another room, I can recollect this one, I can say something about it. But if I go out of this room and fall into an abyss, then I cannot say anything about even this room. So far, with each body, a third point could be caught into words, symbolized, because the body beyond it was there. You could go there and look backward. But only up to the seventh is this possible. Beyond the seventh body nothing can be said, because the seventh is the last body; beyond it is "bodilessness."

With the seventh, one has to choose being or nonbeing – either the language of negation or the language of positivity. And there are only two choices. One is Buddha's choice: he says, "Nothing remains," and the other is Shankara's choice: he says, "Everything remains."

In the seven dimensions – in the seven bodies – as far as man is concerned and as far as the world is concerned, life energy manifests into multidimensional realms. Everywhere, wherever life is to be found, the incoming and the outgoing process will be there. Wherever life is, the process will be. Life cannot exist without this polarity.

So *prana* is energy, cosmic energy, and our first acquaintance with it is in the physical body. It manifests first as breath, and then it goes on manifesting as breath in other forms: influences, magnetism, thoughts, life, creation, being. It goes on, and if one becomes aware of it, one always transcends it to reach to a third point. The moment you reach this third point, you transcend that body and enter the next body. You enter the second body from the first, and so on.

If you go on transcending, up to the seventh there is still a body, but beyond the seventh there is bodilessness. Then you become pure. Then you are not divided; then there are no more polarities. Then it is *advait*, not two: then it is oneness.

CHAPTER 5

Sleep and Wakefulness in the Chakras

Each chakra has a sleep part, except the last – the *sahasrar*. At the seventh chakra, awareness is total: it is pure awareness. That's why Krishna says in the Gita: "The yogi never sleeps." "The yogi" means one who has come to the last center of his being, to the ultimate flowering; one who has become a lotus. He never sleeps. His body sleeps, his mind sleeps: he never sleeps. Even when a buddha is sleeping, deep in the innermost core of his being a light goes on burning bright.

The seventh chakra has no sleep part to it, all the other six chakras have both: yin, yang. Sometimes they sleep and sometimes they are awake: day, night – they have both aspects. When you feel hungry, the center for hunger is awake. If you have ever tried fasting, you would have been surprised. If you try fasting, then for two, three days in the beginning you will feel hunger, and then sometimes hunger will disappear completely. It will come again, it will disappear again, it will come again... You are not eating at all, so you cannot say, "The hunger disappears because I have eaten." You are fasting: sometimes hunger comes with great power, tries to overpower you – and if you remain undisturbed by it, the hunger goes. The chakra has fallen asleep – it will awake again in its turn when the day will come; and it will fall back into sleep again.

The same happens with the sex center. You feel so hungry for love, then you have made love – and then suddenly all desire for love disappears. The chakra has fallen asleep. If you try celibacy, without repression, then you will be surprised. If you don't repress your sexual desire, you simply watch it… Try it for three months – just be watchful. When the desire comes, sit silently, let it be there, let it knock on your doors, listen to it, be attentive – but don't be carried away by it. Let it be there: don't repress it, and don't indulge in it. Be a witness – and you will be surprised again. Sometimes the desire comes with such intensity that one feels one may go crazy. And then automatically on its own accord it disappears, and sex becomes irrelevant. Again it comes, again it disappears. The chakra goes on moving: sometimes it is day, then sex arises; sometimes it is night, then the sex goes to sleep.

And so is true about all six chakras below the seventh. Sleep does not have a separate chakra; sleep has a counterpart with each chakra, except *sahasrar*. So one more thing to be understood: as you grow higher and higher in your chakras, you will have a better quality of sleep because a higher chakra has a deeper quality of relaxation. The man who lives with the first – *muladhar* – will not have a deep sleep. His sleep will be very superficial because he lives with the physical, the material.

I can describe these chakras in this way too. First, the material – *muladhar*. Second, the vital – *svadhishthan*. Third, the sexual, the electrical – *manipura*. Fourth, the moral, aesthetic – *anahata*. Fifth, the religious – *vishuddha*. Sixth, the spiritual – *agya*. And seventh, the divine – *sahasrar*.

As you move higher, your sleep will go deeper and will have

a new quality to it. The man who is food-obsessed and lives only to eat and eat and eat, his sleep will be very disturbed. His sleep will not have silence, peace to it; his sleep will not have music in it. His sleep will be nightmarish. The man who is a little higher than the food addict, who is more interested in people than in things and wants to absorb people, will have a deeper sleep – but not very deep. The sexual person will have the deepest, in the lower realm. That's why sex is used almost as a tranquilizer. If you cannot fall asleep, make love – and immediately you will be falling asleep. Love relieves you of tensions. In the West, doctors go on prescribing sex for those who suffer from sleeplessness. Now they even prescribe sex for people who are prone to heart attacks because sex relaxes, gives you deep sleep.

On the lowest plane, sex gives you the deepest sleep. Then if you move still higher, with the fourth – *anahata* – sleep becomes tremendously tranquil, silent, very purifying and refined. When you love somebody, your relaxation is tremendous, immense. Just the idea that somebody loves you and you love somebody, relaxes you; all tensions are gone. The world is no longer alien, it is a home. With love, the house is transformed into a home and the alien world becomes a community, and nothing is far away. Through the person you love, God has come very much closer. A loving person knows a deep sleep. Hate, and you will miss your sleep. Be angry, and you will miss your sleep – you will fall lower. Love, have compassion, and you will have a deep sleep.

With the fifth, sleep becomes almost prayerful. Hence, all the religions of the world have been insisting to pray before you go to sleep. Let prayer be associated with sleep. Never fall into sleep without prayer, so the rhythm of prayer goes on vibrating in your sleep. The reverberations of the prayer will transform your sleep. The fifth is the center of prayer – and if you can pray, and if you can fall asleep praying, you will be surprised in the morning: you will awake, and you will awake praying. Your very wakefulness will be a sort of prayer. With the fifth, sleep becomes prayer. It is no longer ordinary sleep. You are not only going into sleep, you are going in a subtle way into God.

Sleep is a door when you forget your ego; and it is easier to drop into God than while you are awake, because when you are awake the ego is very strong. When you fall deep into sleep your healing powers function to their total optimum capacity. Hence the physicians say that if a person is ill and cannot sleep, there is no possibility for his being healed – because healing comes from within. Healing comes when the ego is absolutely nonexistential: when the ego is not, then the healing power flows from the within – it wells up. The man who has moved to the fifth, the *vishuddha* chakra – to the chakra of prayer – his life becomes a benediction. You can see: even if he walks you will feel the quality of relaxation in his gestures, in his movements.

The sixth chakra – *agya* – is the last, where sleep becomes perfect, beyond which sleep is not needed: the work is finished. Up to the sixth, sleep is needed. With the sixth, sleep becomes meditative – not even prayerful but meditative – because in prayer there is a duality: I and thou, the devotee and the deity. With the sixth, even that duality disappears. Sleep is profound – as profound as death. In fact, death is nothing but a great sleep, and sleep is nothing but a small death. With the sixth, sleep penetrates to your deepest core and then the work is finished. When you come out of the sixth to the seventh, sleep is no longer needed. You have gone beyond duality. Then you are never tired, so sleep is not needed.

This state of the seventh is the state of pure absolute awareness – call it the state of Christ, Buddha, God.

Somebody has asked a question related to this:

> If sex changes into love, does the urge to dominate
> become will, or the effort to be conscious?

This too has to be understood. The first three lower centers are deeply related with the second part – the three higher centers. First, *muladhar*, *svadhishthan*, *manipura*: these are the first three. The second three are: *anahata*, *vishuddha*, *agya*. These are the two pairs. They are joined together deeply, and it has to be understood – it will be helpful for you, for your journey.

The first chakra is concerned with food and the fourth chakra is concerned with love. Love and food are deeply related, joined together. Hence it happens that whenever somebody loves you, you don't eat much. If a woman is loved she remains lean, thin and beautiful. If she is not loved she starts becoming fat, ugly, goes on accumulating; she starts eating too much. Or, vice versa too: if a woman does not want to be loved, she starts eating too much. That becomes a protection – then nobody will be attracted toward her.

Have you seen? If a beloved comes to your home, a friend has come, and you are so happy, so full of love – that day, appetite disappears. You don't feel like eating – as if something more subtle than food has fulfilled you, something more subtle than food is inside you and the emptiness is not there. You are full, you feel full. Miserable people eat too much, happy people don't eat too much. The happier a person, the less he is addicted to food – because he has a higher food available: love. Love is food on a higher plane. If food is food for the body, love is food for the spirit.

Now even scientists are suspecting it. When a child is born, the mother can give just milk, bodily food. She may not give love – then the child will suffer; his body will grow but his spirit will suffer. Just bodily nourishment is not enough: spiritual nourishment is needed. If a mother only gives food and not love then she is not a mother, she is only a nurse. And the child will suffer for his whole life – something will remain stuck, not grown, retarded. The child needs food, the child needs love: love is needed even more than food.

Have you seen? If a child is given love, he does not bother about food much. If the mother loves the child, she is always worried that the child is not drinking as much milk as he should. But if the mother is non-loving then the child drinks too much milk. In fact it is difficult to take him away from the breast because the child becomes afraid: love is not there, he has to depend only on physical food – the subtle food is missing.

And this goes on happening in your whole life. Whenever you feel that you are missing love, you go on stuffing your body with food – it becomes a substitute. Whenever people feel empty and they don't have that thrill that love brings, that zest that love brings, that energy that love releases, they start stuffing the body with food. They have fallen back to their childhood; they are in a regressed state.

Children who are given enough love are never addicted much to food. Their spirit is so full: the higher is available – who bothers about the lower?

Remember, all the religions have talked about fasting for a certain reason. Unless you are taken out of your food obsession, prayer will not happen. Hence, fasting gives a great possibility to pray. I am not telling you to become addicted to fasting. I am not telling you to start torturing yourself. But if you are a food addict then fasting is the medicine. If you have been eating too much, bring a balance. Eating too much, you remain too attached to the physical and you cannot fly into the sky. You are too burdened: a little fasting will be helpful. And in fasting, people have observed that prayer becomes very easy, simple; it is no longer a problem. Because when you are not burdened too much by food and the body, the spirit is weightless, can fly: the spirit has wings.

The first and the fourth are related. And my experience is this: if people are helped to be more loving, by and by they forget about food. The old religions insist for fasting, I insist for love – and you can see the connection. The old religions insist for fasting, so that you can be taken away from your too-much-food obsession. I insist for love – my technique is more subtle. Then, without even becoming aware, if you are loving you will be taken away from your food obsession. The old religions sometimes can be dangerous, because the food addict can turn into a fast addict. He can become another sort of neurotic person: first he was eating too much, now he may start starving himself. In both the cases he remains concerned with food.

I have watched many Jaina monks: they continuously think about food. They believe in fasting, they fast, but they are continuously thinking about food – what to eat, what not to eat, how to eat, when to eat – their whole psychology is based on food. Food becomes too much of a problem. Hence, I don't insist on fasting, I insist on love – and fasting comes as a shadow. If you are tremendously in love, one day you will find you don't want to eat. The love is so much, and you don't want to destroy it. You are flowing so high, you don't want to stuff yourself and bring yourself low; you don't want to move on earth today. And the fasting comes naturally – you don't think about it, you don't take a vow about it, you don't take a decision about it: suddenly you feel that higher food is available and the lower is not needed – and the fasting happens. Then fasting is beautiful.

The second chakra is related to the fifth. The second chakra is political – domination, domination over others – and the fifth chakra is spiritual power – domination over oneself. With the second chakra you try to overpower people, with the fifth you try to overpower yourself. With the second you try to conquer others, with the fifth you try to conquer yourself. With the second you become a politician, with the fifth you become a priest. And priests and politicians have always remained together: there is a conspiracy between the priest and the politician. The kings and the priests, the politicians and the popes – they are joined together. They may not be aware, but this is the basic cause behind it: the politician needs the support of the priest, and the priest feels somehow in tune with the politician, because both hanker for power – one over others, the other over oneself, but the goal is power.

Remember, I would not like you to become a politician and I would not like you to become a priest either. In fact there is no need to dominate others and there is no need to dominate oneself. Domination as such should be dropped: one should simply be. The very idea of dominating is egoistic – whether you dominate others or yourself makes no difference. Have you not observed that a person who feels that he has great self-control becomes a great egoist? He goes on declaring that he has tremendous control over himself. His ego is strengthened – there is danger.

Domination as such has to be dropped. You should not become a priest. Become religious – don't become a priest. To become religious is one thing, to become a priest is another. The priest by and by starts declaring that he not only has power over himself, he has power over God. The priest by and by starts declaring that he has power over spiritual forces, psychic forces, occult, esoteric. He becomes more and more obsessed with inner powers. But *all* power is an ego trip.

Be aware of the second, and be aware of the fifth too: there are pitfalls, there are dangerous possibilities. And once a person becomes a priest he stops; his growth is no longer going on. Once you have become a priest you are no longer religious; your whole energy has become stagnant. The religious person is always flowing: from first to second, from second to third, from third to fourth, he is always flowing. Up to the seventh, he knows no stopping – there is no station on the way. And with the seventh, he also does not stop because with the seventh, he disappears. There is nobody to stop.

Up to the sixth, you can stop and become stagnant. With each center there is a possibility that you may fall and become stagnant. If you become stagnant with the first, you will know only the material. If you become stagnant with the second, you will know only the political. If you become stagnant with the third, you will know only the sexual – and so on and so forth. The second and fifth are joined together, and so are the third and sixth. The third is the sex center and the sixth is the Tantra center.

Now, one thing to always be remembered: if you are not very alert, you may go on believing that you are moving into Tantra and you may be simply rationalizing your sexuality – it may be nothing but sex, rationalized in the terminology of Tantra. If you move into sex with awareness, it can turn into Tantra. If you move into Tantra with unawareness, it can fall and become ordinary sex. It has happened in India – because only India has tried it.

All the Tantra schools in India, sooner or later, were reduced to sex orgies. It is very difficult to keep aware – it is almost impossible to keep aware. If from the very beginning the discipline has not gone very deep in you, there is every possibility that you will start deceiving yourself. Tantra schools arose in India with great energy, with great insight. And they had something – because that is the last center humanly available: the seventh is superhuman, the seventh is divine. The sixth is the spiritual center.

From sex to Tantra: a great revolution, a mutation, is possible in man. And in the East, people became aware that if you become meditative while making love, the quality of sex changes and something new enters it – it becomes tantric, it becomes prayerful, it becomes meditative. It becomes *samadhi*. And a natural flow happens: from the third you can jump to the sixth – you can bypass the fourth and the fifth. It is a great temptation, a great leap – you can bypass, a shortcut – but dangerous too because you may be simply deceiving yourself. Man is very clever – very clever in finding rationalizations.

I have heard…

From the diary of a globe-trotting young cinema queen:
Monday: The Captain saw me on deck and was kind enough to ask me to sit at his table for the rest of the trip.
Tuesday: I spent the morning on the bridge with the Captain.

He took my picture leaning against the "Passengers not allowed on this bridge" sign.

Wednesday: The Captain made proposals to me, unbecoming an officer and a gentleman.

Thursday: The Captain threatened to sink the ship unless I agreed to his proposals.

Friday: I saved eight hundred lives today.

You can find rationalizations. The temptation is always there – you can find good reasons for wrong motives.

Tantra can any moment become just a garbed sexuality; just nothing but sexuality, in the guise of Tantra,. Then it is dangerous, more dangerous than ordinary sex – ordinary sex is at least honest. You don't pretend, you don't claim something higher; you simply say it is ordinary sex. But Tantra can be dangerous: you start pretending that it is something higher, something superhuman, something not of this world. Keep this in mind. The third and the sixth are very deeply related. The third can become the sixth, the sixth can fall into the third. A great awareness is needed.

These first three and the last three are two balancing forces. The seventh is beyond. When the first three have been balanced by the second three – when the lower has been balanced by the higher, when the lower has been canceled by the higher, when the lower and the higher are of the same weight – then the seventh happens. Then suddenly the duality disappears. Then there is nothing lower, nothing higher; nothing outer, nothing inner; nothing worldly, nothing otherworldly: then only one is. That one is the goal of all search.

CHAPTER 6

The Experience of Death and Life in the Subtle Bodies

The soul resides within two bodies – the subtle body and the gross body. At the time of death, the gross body dies. The body which is made of earth and water, the body which consists of flesh, bones and marrow, drops, dies. Subsequently, the body comprised of subtle thoughts, subtle feelings, subtle vibrations, subtle filaments, remains. This body, formed of all these subtle things, along with the soul, once again proceeds on a journey, and again enters a gross body for a new birth. When a new soul enters the mother's womb, it means this subtle body enters.

In the event of death only the gross body disintegrates, not the subtle body. But with the occurrence of the ultimate death, what we call *moksha*, the subtle body disintegrates along with the gross body. Then there is no more birth for the soul. Then the soul becomes one with the whole. This happens only once. It is like a drop merging into the ocean.

Three things have to be understood. First, there is the element of the soul. When the two types of bodies – the gross and the subtle – come in contact with this element of the soul, both become active. We are familiar with the gross, the physical body; a yogi is familiar with the subtle body, and those who go beyond yoga are familiar with the soul.

Ordinary eyes are able to see the gross body. The yogic eye is able to see the subtle body. But that which is beyond yoga, that which exists beyond the subtle body, is experienced only in *samadhi*. One who goes beyond meditation attains *samadhi*, and it is in the state of *samadhi* that one experiences the divine. The ordinary man has the experience of the physical body, the ordinary yogi has the experience of the subtle body, the enlightened yogi has the experience of the divine. Godliness is one, but there are countless subtle bodies and there are countless gross bodies.

The subtle body is the causal body; it is this body that takes on the new physical body. You see many light bulbs around here. The electricity is one, that energy is one, but it is manifesting through different bulbs. The bulbs have different bodies, but their soul is one. Similarly, the consciousness manifesting through us is one, but in the manifestation of this consciousness, two vehicles are applied. One is the subtle vehicle, the subtle body; the other is the gross vehicle, the gross body.

Our experience is limited to the gross, to the physical body. This restricted experience is the cause of all human misery and ignorance. But there are people who, even after going beyond the physical body, may stop at the subtle body. They will say, "There are an infinite number of souls." But those who go beyond even the subtle body will say, "Godliness is one, the soul is one, *brahman* is one."

When I referred to the entering of the soul, I meant that soul which is still associated with the subtle body. It means the subtle body the soul is enveloped in has not disintegrated yet. That's why we say that the soul which attains to the ultimate freedom steps out of the cycle of birth and death. There is indeed no birth and death for the soul – it was never born, nor will it ever die. The cycle of birth and death stops with the end of the subtle body, because it is the subtle body that causes a new birth.

The subtle body is an integrated seed consisting of our thoughts, desires, lusts, longings, experiences, knowledge. This body is instrumental in taking us on our continuing journey. However, one whose thoughts are all annihilated, whose passions have all vanished, whose desires have all disappeared, who has no desire left within him, there is no place for him to go, there is no reason left for him to go anywhere. Then there is no reason for him to take birth again.

There is a wonderful story in the life of Ramakrishna. Those who were close to him, who knew him to be a *paramahansa*, an enlightened one, used to be deeply troubled about one thing. It bothered them greatly to see an enlightened person such as Ramakrishna – one who had attained *samadhi* – craving food so much. Ramakrishna used to become very anxious about food. He would often enter the kitchen, asking his wife Sharda Devi, "What's cooking today? It's getting so late!" Right in the middle of a serious talk on spiritual matters, he would get up abruptly and rush toward the kitchen asking what was being cooked, start looking for food.

Feeling embarrassed, Sharda would politely chide him, "What are you doing? What must people think – dropping the talk on *brahman* so suddenly and starting to talk about food!" Ramakrishna would laugh and remain silent.

Even his close disciples remonstrated with him. They would say, "It's giving you a bad name. People say, 'How can such a person have attained knowledge when his desire for food is so overwhelming?'"

One day his wife Sharda got very upset and reproached him. Ramakrishna told her, "You have no idea, but the day I show an aversion to food, know that I shall not live more than three days afterward."

Sharda asked, "What do you mean?"

Ramakrishna said, "All my desires and passions have disappeared, all my thoughts are gone – but for the good of mankind I am deliberately holding on to this one desire for food. It's like a boat tied down with one last rope. Once that rope is cut loose, the boat will move on to its endless journey. I am staying on with effort."

Perhaps those around him did not give much thought to this at the time. But three days before Ramakrishna's death, when Sharda entered with a dish of food, Ramakrishna looked at it, shut his eyes, and lay with his back turned toward her. In a flash she remembered Ramakrishna's words about his death. The dish fell from her hands and she began to weep bitterly. Ramakrishna said, "Don't cry. You wished I should not crave for food – your wish has come true."

Exactly three days after this incident Ramakrishna died. He was holding on with effort to just a little bit of desire. That little desire had become the support for the continuation of his life journey. With the disappearance of that desire, the entire support ceased to exist.

Those whom we call the *tirthankaras*, those whom we call the buddhas, the sons of God, the *avatars* – they hold on to only one desire. They keep the desire solely out of compassion, for the good and well-being of all mankind. The day this desire is lost, they cease to live in the body and an endless journey toward the infinite begins. After that there is no more birth, no more death. After that there is neither one nor many. What remains after that cannot, in any way, be counted in numbers; hence those who know don't even say, "*Brahman* is one, the divine is one." To call it "one" is meaningless when there is no way to follow it with "two," when one can't count any further in the sequence of two and three. Saying "one" is meaningful only as long as two, three and four are also there. "One" is significant only in the context of other numbers. That's why those who know don't even say *brahman* is one; they say *brahman* is non-dual, he is not two.

They are saying something quite remarkable. They are saying, "Godliness is not two; there is no way you can count godliness in terms of numbers." Even calling it one we are attempting to count it in terms of numbers, which is wrong. But to experience that one is still a long way. Right now we are still at the level of the gross body, of the body which endlessly takes multiple forms. When we enter this body we find another body – the subtle body. Going beyond this subtle body, we attain that which is not a body, that which is bodiless – the soul.

PART II

DIFFERENT MAPS FOR DIFFERENT PATHS

CHAPTER 7

The Heart Sutra and the Path of Buddha

Homage to the perfection of wisdom, the lovely, the holy!

Avalokita, the holy lord and bodhisattva, was moving in the deep course of the wisdom which has gone beyond. He looked down from on high, he beheld but five heaps, and he saw that in their own being they were empty.

I salute the buddha within you. You may not be aware of it, you may not have ever dreamed about it – that you are a buddha, that nobody can be anything else, that buddhahood is the very essential core of your being, that it is not something to happen in the future, that it has happened already. It is the very source you come from; it is the source and the goal too. It is from buddhahood that we move, and it is to buddhahood that we move. This one word, *buddhahood*, contains all – the full circle of life, from the alpha to the omega.

But you are fast asleep, you don't know who you are. Not

that you have to become a buddha, but only that you have to recognize it, that you have to return to your own source, that you have to look within yourself. A confrontation with yourself will reveal your buddhahood. The day one comes to see oneself, the whole of existence becomes enlightened. It is not that a person becomes enlightened – how can a person become enlightened? The very idea of being a person is part of the unenlightened mind. It is not that I have become enlightened; the "I" has to be dropped before one can become enlightened, so how can I become enlightened? That is absurdity. The day I became enlightened, the whole of existence became enlightened. Since that moment I have not seen anything other than buddhas – in many forms, with many names, with a thousand and one problems, but buddhas still.

So I salute the buddha within you.

I am immensely glad that so many buddhas have gathered here. The very fact of your coming here to me is the beginning of the recognition. The respect in your heart for me, the love in your heart for me, is respect and love for your own buddhahood. The trust in me is not a trust in something extrinsic to you, the trust in me is self-trust. By trusting me, you will learn to trust yourself. By coming close to me, you will come close to yourself. Only a recognition has to be attained. The diamond is there – you have forgotten about it, or you have never remembered it from the very beginning.

There is a very famous saying of Emerson: "Man is a God in ruins." I agree and I disagree. The insight has some truth in it – man is not as he should be. The insight is there but a little upside down. Man is not God in ruins, man is God in the making; man is a budding buddha. The bud is there, it can bloom any moment: just a little effort, just a little help is needed. And the help is not going to cause it – it is already there! Your effort is only going to reveal it to you, help to unfold what is there, hidden. It is a discovery, but the truth is already there. The truth is eternal.

Listen to these sutras because these are the most important sutras in the great Buddhist literature. Hence they are called the *Heart Sutra*; it is the very heart of the Buddhist message.

But I would like to begin from the very beginning. From this point only does Buddhism become relevant: let it be there in your heart that you are a buddha. I know it may look presumptuous, it may look very hypothetical; you cannot trust it totally. That is natural, I understand it. Let it be there, but as a seed. Around that fact many things will start happening, and only around that fact will you be able to understand these sutras. They are immensely powerful – very small, very condensed, seedlike. But with this soil, with the vision in the mind that you are a buddha, that you are a budding buddha, that you are potentially capable of becoming one, that nothing is lacking, all is ready, things just have to be put in the right order, that a little more awareness is needed, a little more consciousness is needed… The treasure is there; you have to bring a small lamp inside your house. Once the darkness disappears you will no longer be a beggar, you will be a buddha; you will be a sovereign, an emperor. This whole kingdom is yours and it is just for the asking; you have just to claim it.

But you cannot claim it if you believe that you are a beggar. You cannot claim it, you cannot even dream about claiming if you think that you are a beggar. This idea that you are a beggar, that you are ignorant, that you are a sinner, has been preached from so many pulpits down the ages that it has become a deep hypnosis in you. This hypnosis has to be broken. To break it, I start with: I salute the buddha within you.

To me, you are buddhas. All your efforts to become enlightened are ridiculous if you don't accept this basic fact. This has to become a tacit understanding, that you *are* it! This is the right beginning, otherwise you go astray. This is the right beginning. Start with this vision, and don't be worried that this may create some kind of ego: "I am a buddha." Don't be worried, because the whole process of the *Heart Sutra* will make it clear to you that the ego is the only thing that doesn't exist – the *only* thing that doesn't exist! Everything else is real.

There have been teachers who say the world is illusory and the soul is existential – the "I" is true and all else is illusory, maya. Buddha says just the reverse: he sees only the "I" is untrue and everything else is real. And I agree with Buddha more than with the other standpoint. Buddha's insight is very penetrating, the most penetrating. Nobody has ever penetrated those realms, depths and heights of reality.

But start with the idea, with this climate around you, with this vision. Let it be declared to every cell of your body and every thought of your mind; let it be declared to every nook and corner of your existence: "I am a buddha!" And don't be worried about the "I," we will take care of it.

"I" and buddhahood cannot exist together. Once the buddhahood becomes revealed the "I" disappears, just like darkness disappears when you bring a light in.

Before entering the sutras, it will be helpful to understand a little framework, a little structure.

The ancient Buddhist scriptures talk about seven temples. Just as Sufis talk about seven valleys, and Hindus talk about seven chakras, the Buddhists talk about seven temples.

The first temple is the physical, the second temple is psychosomatic, the third temple is psychological, the fourth temple is psycho-spiritual, the fifth temple is spiritual, the sixth temple is spirituo-transcendental, and the seventh temple and the ultimate – the temple of temples – is the transcendental.

The sutras belong to the seventh. These are declarations of someone who has entered the seventh temple, the transcendental, the absolute. That is the meaning of the Sanskrit word, *pragyaparamita* – the wisdom of the beyond, from the beyond, in the beyond; the wisdom that comes only when you have transcended all kinds of identifications – lower or higher, this worldly

or that worldly; when you have transcended all kinds of identifications, when you are not identified at all, when there is only a
pure flame of awareness left with no smoke around it. That's why
Buddhists worship this small book, this very, very small book;
and they have called it the *Heart Sutra* – the very heart of religion,
the very core.

The first temple, the physical, can correspond to the Hindu
map with the *muladhar* chakra; the second, the psychosomatic,
with *svadhisthan* chakra; the third, the psychological, with *manipura*; the fourth, the psycho-spiritual, with *anahata*; the fifth, the
spiritual, with *vishuddh*; the sixth, the spirituo-transcendental, with
agya; and the seventh, the transcendental, with *sahasrar*. *Sahasrar*
means the one-thousand-petaled lotus. That is the symbol of the
ultimate flowering: nothing has remained hidden, all has become
unhidden, manifest. The thousand-petaled lotus has opened and
the whole sky is filled with its fragrance, its beauty, its benediction.

In the modern world, a great work has started in search of
the innermost core of the human being. It will be good to understand how far modern efforts lead us.

Pavlov, B. F. Skinner and the other behaviorists, go on cir-
cling around the physical, the *muladhar*. They think man is only
the body. They get so involved in the first temple, they get so
involved with the physical that they forget everything else. These
people are trying to explain man only through the physical, the
material. This attitude becomes a hindrance because they are
not open. When from the very beginning you deny that there
is anything other than the body, then you deny the explo-
ration itself. This becomes a prejudice. A Communist, a Marxist,
a behaviorist, an atheist – people who believe that man is only
the body – their very belief closes the doors to higher realities.
They become blind. And the physical is there, the physical is the
most apparent; it needs no proof. The physical body is there,
you need not prove it. Because it need not be proved, it becomes
the only reality. That is nonsense. Then man loses all dignity. If

there is nothing to grow in or to grow toward, there cannot be any dignity in life. Then man becomes a thing. Then you are not an opening, then nothing more is going to happen to you – you are a body: you will eat and you will defecate, and you will eat and you will make love and produce children, and this will go on and on, and one day you will die. A mechanical repetition of the mundane, the trivia – how can there be any significance, any meaning, any poetry? How can there be any dance?

Skinner has written a book, *Beyond Freedom and Dignity*. It should be called *Below Freedom and Dignity*, not *Beyond*. It is below, it is the lowest standpoint about man, the ugliest. There is nothing wrong with the body, remember. I am not against the body, it is a beautiful temple. The ugliness enters when you think it is all.

Man can be conceived of as a ladder with seven rungs, and you become identified with the first rung. Then you are not going anywhere. And the ladder is there, and the ladder bridges this world and the other; the ladder bridges matter with godliness. The first rung is perfectly good if it is used in relationship to the whole ladder. If it functions as a first step it is immensely beautiful: one should be thankful to the body. But if you start worshipping the first rung and you forget the remaining six, you forget that the whole ladder exists and you become closed, confined to the first rung, then it is no longer a rung at all – because a rung is a rung only when it is part of a ladder. If it is no longer a rung then you are stuck with it. Hence, people who are materialistic are always stuck, they always feel something is missing, they don't feel they are going anywhere. They move in rounds, in circles, and they come again and again to the same point. They become tired and bored. They start contemplating how to commit suicide. And their whole effort in life is to find some sensations, so something new can happen. But what "new" can happen? All the things that we go on being occupied with are nothing but toys to play with.

Think of these words of Frank Sheed: "The soul of man is crying for purpose or meaning. And the scientist says, 'Here is a telephone.' Or, 'Look! Television!' – exactly as one tries to distract a baby crying for its mother by offering it sugar sticks and making funny faces at it. The leaping stream of invention has served extraordinarily well to keep man occupied, to keep him from remembering that which is troubling him."

All that the modern world has provided you with is nothing but sugar sticks, toys to play with – and you were crying for your mother, you were crying for love, and you were crying for consciousness, and you were crying for some significance in life. And they say, "Look! The telephone. Look! The television. Look! We have brought so many beautiful things for you." And you play around a little bit; again you become fed up, again you are bored, and again they go on searching for new toys for you to play with.

This state of affairs is ridiculous. It is so absurd that it seems almost inconceivable how we go on living in it. We are caught at the first rung.

Remember that you are in the body, but you are not the body; let that be a continuous awareness in you. You live in the body, and the body is a beautiful abode. Remember, I am not for a single moment hinting that you become anti-body, that you start denying the body as the so-called spiritualists have done down the ages. The materialists go on thinking that the body is all that is, and there are people who move to the opposite extreme, and they start saying that the body is illusory, the body is not: "Destroy the body so the illusion is destroyed, and you can become really real."

This other extreme is a reaction. The materialist creates his own reaction in the spiritualist, but they are partners in the same business; they are not very different people. The body is beautiful, the body is real, the body has to be lived, the body has to be loved. The body is a great gift of existence. Not for a single moment be against it, and not for a single moment think that you are only it. You are far bigger. Use the body as a jumping board.

The second temple is: psychosomatic, *svadhisthan*. Freudian psychoanalysis functions there. It goes a little higher than Skinner and Pavlov. Freud enters the mysteries of the psychological a little bit more. He's not just a behaviorist, but he never goes beyond dreams. He goes on analyzing dreams.

The dream exists as an illusion in you. It is indicative, it is symbolic; it has a message from the unconscious to be revealed to the conscious. But there is no point in just getting caught in it. Use the dream, but don't become the dream. You are not the dream.

And there is no need to make so much fuss about it, as Freudians do. Their whole effort seems to be moving in the dimension of the dream world. Take note of it, take a very, very clear standpoint about it, understand its message; and there is really no need to go to anybody else for your dream analysis. If you cannot analyze your dream, nobody else can because your dream is your dream. And your dream is so personal that nobody else can dream the way you dream. Nobody has ever dreamed the way you dream, nobody will ever dream the way you dream; nobody can explain it to you. His interpretation will be *his* interpretation. Only you can look into it. And in fact there is no need to analyze a dream: look at the dream in its totality, with clarity, with alertness, and you will see the message. It is so loud! There is no need to go for psychoanalysis for three, four, five, seven years.

A person who is dreaming every night, and in the day is going to the psychoanalyst to be analyzed, becomes by and by surrounded by dreamy-stuff. Just as the first becomes too obsessed with the *muladhar*, the physical, the second becomes too obsessed with the sexual – because the second, the realm of psychosomatic reality, is sex. The second starts interpreting everything in terms of sex. Whatsoever you do, go to the

Freudian and he will reduce it to sex. Nothing higher exists for him. He lives in the mud, he does not believe in the lotus. Bring a lotus flower to him, he will look at it and reduce it to the mud. He will say, "This is nothing, this is just dirty mud. Has it not come out of dirty mud? If it has come out of dirty mud, then it has to be dirty mud." Reduce everything to its cause, and that is the real.

Then every poem is reduced to sex, everything beautiful is reduced to sex and perversion and repression. Michelangelo is a great artist? Then his art has to be reduced to some sexuality. And Freudians go to absurd lengths. They say all the great works of art by Michelangelo or Goethe or Byron which bring great joy to millions of people, are nothing but repressed sex – maybe Goethe was going to masturbate and was stopped.

Millions of people are stopped from masturbation, but they don't become Goethes. It is absurd. But Freud is the master of the world of the toilet. He lives there, that is his temple. Art becomes pathology, poetry becomes pathology, everything becomes perversion. If Freudian analysis succeeds, then there will be no Kalidas, no Shakespeare, no Michelangelo, no Mozart, no Wagner, because everybody will be normal. These are abnormal people, these people are psychologically ill, according to Freud. The greatest are reduced to the lowest. Buddha is ill, according to Freud, because whatsoever he is talking about is nothing but repressed sex.

This approach reduces human greatness to ugliness. Beware of it. Buddha is not ill; in fact, Freud is ill. The silence of Buddha, the joy of Buddha, the celebration of Buddha is not ill, it is the full flowering of well-being.

But to Freud the normal person is one who has never sang a song, who has never danced, who has never celebrated, never prayed, never meditated, never done anything creative, is just normal: goes to the office, comes home, eats, drinks, sleeps, and dies; leaves not a trace behind of his creativity, leaves not a single signature anywhere. This normal man seems to be very mediocre, dull, and dead. There is a suspicion about Freud that because he himself could not create – he was an uncreative person – he was condemning creativity itself as pathology. There is every possibility that he was a mediocre person. It is his mediocreness which feels offended by all the great people of the world.

The mediocre mind is trying to reduce all greatness. The mediocre mind cannot accept that there can be any greater being than him. That hurts. This whole psychoanalysis and its interpretation of human life is revenge by the mediocre. Beware of it. It is better than the first, yes, a little ahead of the first, but one has to go, and go on going, beyond and beyond.

The third is psychological. Adler lives in the world of the psychological, the will to power; at least something – very egoistic, but at least something; a little more open than Freud. But the problem is, just like Freud reduces everything to sex, Adler reduces everything to the inferiority complex. People try to become great because they feel inferior. A person trying to become enlightened is a person who is feeling inferior, and a person trying to become enlightened is a person who is on a power trip.

This is utterly wrong, because we have seen people – a Buddha, a Christ, a Krishna – who are so utterly surrendered that their trip cannot be called a power trip. And when Buddha blooms he has no ideas of superiority, not at all. He bows down to the whole of existence. He has not that idea of holier-than-thou, not at all. Everything is holy, even the dust is divine. No, he is not thinking himself superior, and he was not striving to become superior. He was not feeling inferior at all. He was born a king; there was no question of inferiority. He was at the top from the very beginning, there was no question of inferiority. He was the richest man in his country, the most powerful man in his country: there was no more power to be attained, no more riches to be attained. He was one of the most beautiful men ever born on this earth, he had one of the most beautiful women as his beloved. All was available to him.

But Adler would go on searching for some inferiority because he could not believe that a man could have any goal other than the ego. It is better – better than Freud, a little higher. Ego is a little higher than sex; not much higher, but a little.

The fourth is psycho-spiritual, *anahata*, the heart center. Jung, Assagioli and others penetrate that realm. They go higher than Pavlov, Freud and Adler, they open more possibilities. They accept the world of the irrational, the unconscious: they don't confine themselves to reason. They are more reasonable people – they accept "irreason" too. The irrational is not denied but accepted. This is where modern psychology stops – at the fourth rung. And the fourth rung is just in the middle of the whole ladder: three rungs on this side and three rungs on that side.

Modern psychology is not yet a complete science. It is hanging in the middle. It is very shaky, not certain about anything. It is more hypothetical than experiential. It is still struggling to be.

The fifth is spiritual: Islam, Hinduism, Christianity – the mass-organized religions remain stuck with the fifth. They don't go beyond the spiritual. All the organized religions, the churches, remain there.

The sixth is the spirituo-transcendental – yoga and other methods. All over the world, down the ages, many methods have been developed which are less like a church organization, which are not dogmatic but are more experiential. You have to do something with your body and mind; you have to create a certain harmony within yourself so that you can ride on that harmony, you can ride on that cloud of harmony and go far away from your ordinary reality. Yoga can comprehend all that; that is the sixth.

And the seventh is transcendental: Tantra, Tao, Zen. Buddha's attitude is of the seventh – *pragyaparamita*. It means wisdom that is transcendental, wisdom that comes to you only when all the bodies have been crossed and you have become just a pure awareness, just a witness, pure subjectivity.

Unless man reaches the transcendental, he will have to be provided with toys, sugar sticks. He will have to be provided with false meanings.

Just the other day I came across an American car advertisement. On top of a beautiful car it says: "Something to believe in." Man has never fallen so low. Something to believe in! You believe in a car? Yes, people believe – people believe in their houses, people believe in their cars, people believe in their bank balances. If you look around you will be surprised – God has disappeared, but belief has not disappeared. God is no longer there: now there is a Cadillac or a Lincoln! God has disappeared but man has created new gods – Stalin, Mao. God has disappeared and man has created new gods – movie stars.

This is for the first time in the history of human consciousness that man has fallen so low. And even if sometimes you remember God, it is just an empty word. Maybe when you are in pain, maybe when you are frustrated, then you use God – as if God is aspirin. That's what the so-called religions have made you believe: they say, "Take God three times a day and you won't feel any pain!" So whenever you are in pain you remember God. God is not an aspirin, God is not a painkiller.

A few people remember God habitually, a few others remember God professionally. A priest remembers professionally. He has nothing to do with God, he is paid for it. He has become proficient. A few people remember habitually, a few professionally, but nobody seems to remember God in deep love. A few people invoke his name when they are miserable; nobody remembers him when they are in joy, celebrating. And that is the right moment to remember – because only when you are joyous, immensely joyous, are you close to God. When you are in misery you are far away, when you are in misery you are closed. When you are happy you are open, flowing; you can hold God's hand.

So you remember habitually because you have been taught from very childhood – it has become a kind of habit, like smoking. If you smoke you don't enjoy it much; if you don't smoke you feel you are missing something. If you remember God every morning, every evening, nothing is attained because the remembrance is not of the heart – just verbal, mental, mechanical. But if you don't remember, you start feeling something is missing. It has become a ritual. Beware of making God a ritual, and beware of becoming professional about it.

I have heard a very famous story:

The story is about a great yogi, very famous, who was promised by a king that if he could go into deep *samadhi* and remain under the earth for one year, the king would give him the best horse in the kingdom as a reward. The king knew that the yogi had a soft heart for horses, he was a great lover of horses.

The yogi agreed; he was buried alive for a year. But in the course of the year the kingdom was overthrown and nobody remembered to dig up the yogi.

About ten years later someone remembered: "What happened to the yogi?" The king sent a few people to find out. The yogi was dug up; he was still in his deep trance. A previously agreed to mantra was whispered in his ear and he was roused, and the first thing he said was, "Where is my horse?"

Ten years of remaining in silence underneath the earth, but the mind has not changed at all – "Where is my horse?" Was this man really in trance, in *samadhi*? Was he thinking about God? He must have been thinking about the horse. But he was professionally proficient, skillful. He must have learned a technique to stop the breathing and to go into a kind of death – but it was technical.

Remaining ten years in such deep silence, and the mind has not changed a little bit! It is exactly the same as if these ten years had not passed by. If you technically remember God, if you professionally remember God, habitually, mechanically remember

God, then nothing is going to happen. All is possible, but all possibilities go through the heart. Hence the name of this scripture: the *Heart Sutra.*

Unless you do something with great love, with great involvement, with great commitment, with sincerity, with authenticity, with your total being, nothing is going to happen.

For some people religion is like an artificial limb: it has neither warmth nor life. And although it helps them to stumble along, it never becomes part of them; it must be strapped on each day.

Remember, this has happened to millions of people on the earth, this can happen to you too. Don't create an artificial limb, let real limbs grow in you. Only then will your life have a warmth, only then will your life have joy – not a false smile on the lips, not a pseudo kind of happiness that you pretend to, not a mask, but in reality. Ordinarily you go on wearing things: somebody wears a beautiful smile, somebody wears a very compassionate face, somebody wears a very, very loving personality – but these are like clothes that you put on. Deep down you remain the same.

These sutras can become a revolution.

The first thing, the beginning, is always the question, "Who am I?" And one has to go on asking. When first you ask, "Who am I?" the *muladhar* will answer, "You are a body! What nonsense! There is no need to ask, you know it already." Then the second will say, "You are sexuality." Then the third will say, "You are a power trip, an ego" – and so on and so forth.

Remember, you have to stop only when there is no answer coming, not before. If some answer is coming: "You are this, you are this," then know well that some center is providing you with an answer. When all the six centers have been crossed and all their answers canceled, you go on asking, "Who am I?" and no answer comes from anywhere, it is utter silence. Your question resounds in yourself: "Who am I?" and there is silence, no answer arises from anywhere, from any corner. You are absolutely present, absolutely silent, and there is not even a vibration. "Who am I?" – and only silence. Then a miracle happens: you cannot even formulate the question. Answers have become absurd; then finally the question also becomes absurd. First answers disappear, then the question also disappears – because they can live only together. They are like two sides of a coin – if one side has gone, the other cannot be retained. First answers disappear, then the question disappears. And with the disappearance of question and answer, you come to realize: that is transcendental. You know, yet you cannot say; you know, yet you cannot be articulate about it. You know from your very being who you are, but it cannot be verbalized. It is life-knowledge; it is not scriptural, it is not borrowed, it is not from others. It has arisen in you.

And with this arising, you are a buddha. And then you start laughing because you come to know that you have been a buddha from the very beginning; you had just never looked so deep. You were running around and around outside your being, you had never come home.

The philosopher, Arthur Schopenhauer, was walking down a lonely street. Buried in thought, he accidentally bumped into another pedestrian. Angered by the jolt and the apparent unconcern of the philosopher, the pedestrian shouted, "Well! Who do you think you are?"

Still lost in thought the philosopher said, "Who am I? How I wish I knew."

Nobody knows. Knowing this – I don't know who I am – the journey starts.

The first sutra:

Homage to the perfection of wisdom, the lovely, the holy!

This is an invocation. All Indian scriptures start with an

invocation for a certain reason. This is not so in other countries and in other languages; this is not so in Greece. The Indian understanding is that we are hollow bamboos, only the infinite flows through us. The infinite has to be invoked; we become just instruments to it. We invoke it, we call it forth to flow through us. That's why nobody knows who wrote this *Heart Sutra*. It has not been signed because the person who wrote it didn't believe that he was the author of it. He was just instrumental. He was just like a steno; the dictation was from beyond. It was dictated to him, he has faithfully written it, but he is not the author of it – at the most, just the writer.

Homage to the perfection of wisdom, the lovely, the holy! This is the invocation, a few words, but every word is very, very pregnant with meaning.

Homage to the perfection of wisdom… "Perfection of wisdom" is the translation of *pragyaparamita. Pragya* means wisdom. Remember, it does not mean knowledge. Knowledge is that which comes through the mind, knowledge is that which comes from the outside. Knowledge is *never* original. It can't be original, by its very nature; it is borrowed. Wisdom is your original vision: it does not come from the outside, it grows in you. It is not like an artificial plastic flower that you go to the market and purchase. It is a real rose that grows on the tree, through the tree. It is the song of the tree. It comes from its innermost core; it arises from its depth . One day it is unexpressed, another day it is expressed; one day it was unmanifest, another day it has become manifest.

Pragya means wisdom, but in the English language even *wisdom* has a different connotation. In English, *knowledge* means without experience: you go to the university, you gather knowledge. *Wisdom* means you go to life and you gather experience. So a young man can be knowledgeable but never wise, because wisdom needs time. A young man can have degrees: he can be a PhD or a DLitt – that is not difficult – but only an old man can be wise. *Wisdom* means knowledge gathered through one's own experience, but it is still from the outside.

Pragya is neither knowledge nor wisdom as ordinarily understood. It is a flowering within – not through experience, not through others, not through life and life's encounters, no, but just by going within in utter silence, and allowing that which is hidden there to explode. You are carrying wisdom as a seed within you; it just needs the right soil so that it can sprout. Wisdom is always original. It is always yours, and only yours.

But remember again, when I say "yours" I don't mean that there is any ego involved in it. It is yours in the sense that it comes out of your self-nature, but it has no claim to the ego – because again ego is part of the mind, not of your inner silence. *Paramita* means of the beyond, from the beyond, beyond time and space; when you move to a state where time disappears, when you move to an inner place where space disappears, when you don't know where you are and when, when both references have disappeared. Time is outside you, so is space outside you. There is a crossing point within you where time disappears.

Somebody asked Jesus, "Tell us something about the kingdom of God. What will be special there?" Jesus is reported to have said, "There will be time no longer." There is eternity, a timeless moment. That is the beyond – a spaceless space and a timeless moment. You are no longer confined, so you cannot say where you are.

Now look at me: I cannot say I am here, because I am there too. And I cannot say I am in India, because I am in China too. And I cannot say that I am on this planet, because I am not. When the ego disappears you are simply one with the whole. You are everywhere *and* nowhere. You don't exist as a separate entity, you are dissolved.

Look! In the morning, on a beautiful leaf, there is a dewdrop shining in the morning sun, utterly beautiful. And then it starts slipping, and it slips into the ocean. It was there on the leaf: there was time and space, it had a definition, a personality of its own. Now once it has dropped into the ocean you cannot find it anywhere – not because it has become nonexistential, no. Now it is everywhere; that's why you cannot find it anywhere. You cannot locate it because the whole ocean has become its location. Now it doesn't exist separately.

When you don't exist in separation from the whole, there arises *pragyaparamita*, the wisdom that is perfect, the wisdom that is from the beyond.

Homage to the perfection of wisdom, the lovely, the holy! A beautiful provocation. It says: my homage is to the wisdom that comes when you move into the beyond. And it is lovely, and it is holy – holy because you have become one with the whole; lovely because the ego that created all kinds of ugliness in your life is no more.

Satyam, *shivam*, *sundaram*: it is true, it is good, it is beautiful. These are the three qualities.

Homage to the perfection of wisdom… Truth… That's what truth is: the perfection of wisdom, the lovely, the beautiful, the holy, the good.

Why is it called holy? – because buddhas are born out of it. It is the womb of the buddhas. You become a buddha the moment you partake of this perfection of wisdom. You become a buddha when the dewdrop disappears into the ocean, loses separation, is no longer struggling against the whole, is surrendered, is with the whole, no longer against it. Hence my insistence to be with nature, never against it. Never try to overcome it, never try to conquer it, never try to defeat it. If you try to defeat it, you are doomed to failure because the part cannot defeat the whole – and that's what everybody is trying to do. Hence there is so much frustration, because everybody seems to be a failure. Everybody is trying to conquer the whole, trying to push the river. Naturally you become tired one day, exhausted – you have a very limited source of energy; the river is vast. One day it takes you, but you give in, in frustration.

If you can give in joyfully, it becomes surrender. Then it is no longer defeat, it is a victory. You win only with existence, never against existence. And remember, existence is not trying to defeat you. Your defeat is self-generated. You are defeated because you fight. If you want to be defeated, fight; if you want to win, surrender. This is the paradox: those who are ready to give in become the winners. The losers are the only winners in this game. Try to win and your defeat is absolutely certain – it is only a question of time, of when, but it is certain it is going to happen.

It is holy because you are one with the whole. You throb with it, you dance with it, you sing with it. You are like a leaf in the wind: the leaf simply dances with the wind, it has no will of its own. This will-lessness is what I call sannyas, what the sutra calls holy.

The Sanskrit word for holy is *bhagavati*. That is even more important to be understood than the word *holy* because the word *holy* may carry some Christian connotation to it. *Bhagavati* is feminine for *bhagavan*. First, the sutra did not use the word *bhagavan*, it used *bhagavati*, the feminine – because the source of all is feminine, not masculine. It is yin, not yang, it is a mother, not a father.

The Christian concept of God as the father is not so beautiful. It is nothing but male ego. The male ego cannot think that God can be a "she"; the male ego wants God to be a "he." And you see the whole Christian trinity: all three are men, woman is not included there – God the father, and Christ the son, and the Holy Ghost. It is an all-male club. And remember well that the feminine is far more fundamental in life than the man, because only the woman has a womb; only the woman can give birth to life, to new life. It comes through the feminine.

Why does it come through the feminine? It is not just accidental. It comes through the feminine because only the feminine can allow it to come – because the feminine is receptive. The masculine is aggressive; the feminine can receive, absorb, can become a passage.

The Sanskrit sutra says *bhagavati*, not *bhagavan*. It is of immense importance. That perfect wisdom out of which all the buddhas come is a feminine element, a mother. The womb has to be a mother. Once you think of God as the father, you don't seem to understand what you are doing. The father is an unnatural institution. The father does not exist in nature. The father has existed only for a few thousand years; it is a human institution. The mother exists everywhere, the mother is natural.

The father came into the world because of private property. The father is part of economics, not of nature. And once private property disappears – if it ever disappears – the father will disappear. The mother will remain there always and always. We cannot conceive of a world without the mother, we can conceive of a world without the father very easily. And the very idea is aggressive. Have you not seen? Only Germans call their country the "fatherland," every other country calls it the "motherland." These are dangerous people! "Motherland" is okay. By calling your country the "fatherland" you are starting something dangerous, you are putting something dangerous on foot. Sooner or later the aggression will come, the war will come. The seed is there.

All the religions that have thought of God as the father have been aggressive religions. Christianity is aggressive, so is Islam. And you know perfectly well that the Jewish God is a very angry and arrogant God. The Jewish God declares: "If you are not for me, then you are against me and I will destroy you. And I am a very jealous God; only worship me!" The people who have thought of God as the mother have been nonviolent people.

Buddhists have never fought a war in the name of religion. They have never tried to convert a single human being by any force, by coercion of whatsoever sort. Mohammedans have tried to convert people with the sword, against their will, against their conscience, against their consciousness. Christians have tried to manipulate people to become Christians in all kinds of ways – sometimes through the sword, sometimes through bread, sometimes through other persuasions. Buddhism is the only religion that has not converted a single human being against his conscience. Only Buddhism is a nonviolent religion, because the concept of the ultimate reality is feminine.

Homage to the perfection of wisdom, the lovely, the holy! Remember, truth is beautiful. Truth is beauty because truth is a benediction. Truth cannot be ugly, and the ugly cannot be true; the ugly is illusory.

When you see an ugly person, don't be deceived by his ugliness; search a little deeper and you will find a beautiful person hidden there. Don't be deceived by ugliness. Ugliness is in your interpretation. Life is beautiful, truth is beautiful, existence is beautiful – it knows no ugliness.

It is lovely, it is feminine, and it is holy. But remember, what is meant by holy is not what is ordinarily meant – as if it is otherworldly, as if it is sacred against the mundane and the profane, no. All is holy. There is nothing which can be called mundane or profane. All is sacred because all is suffused with one.

There are buddhas and buddhas! – buddha-trees and buddha-dogs and buddha-birds and buddha-men and buddha-women – but all are buddhas. All are on the way. Man is not God in ruins, man is God in the making, on the way.

The second sutra:

Avalokita, the holy lord and bodhisattva, was moving in the deep course of the wisdom which has gone beyond.
He looked down from on high, he beheld but five heaps, and he saw that in their own being they were empty.

Avalokita is a name of Buddha. Literally it means one who looks from above – *avalokita* – one who looks from above, one who stands at the seventh center, *sahasrar*, the transcendental, and looks from there. Naturally, whatsoever you see is contaminated by your standpoint, is contaminated by the space you are in.

If a man who lives at the first rung – the physical body – looks at anything, he looks from that standpoint. A man who lives at the physical only looks at your body when he looks at you, he cannot look at more than that, he cannot see more than that. Your vision of things depends on from where you are looking.

A man who is sexually disturbed, sexually involved in fantasies, only looks from that standpoint. A man who is hungry looks from that standpoint. Watch in your own self. You look at things, and each time you look at things they appear different because you are different. In the morning the world looks a little more beautiful than in the evening. In the morning you are fresh, and in the morning you have come from a depth of great sleep, the deep sleep, the dreamless sleep. You have tasted something of the transcendental, although unconsciously. So in the morning everything looks beautiful. People are more compassionate, more loving; people are purer in the morning, people are more innocent in the morning. By the time evening arrives those same people will become more corrupted, more cunning, clever, manipulating, ugly, violent, deceiving. They are the same people, but in the morning they were very close to the transcendental. By the evening they have lived in the mundane, in the worldly, in the physical too much, and they have become focused there.

The man of perfection is one who can move through all these seven chakras easily – that is the man of freedom – who is not fixed at any point, who is like a dial: you can adjust it to any vision. That is what is called a *mukta*, one who is really free. He can move in all the dimensions and yet remain untouched by them. His purity is never lost, his purity remains of the transcendental.

Buddha can come and touch your body and heal your body. He can become a body, but that is his freedom. He can become a mind and he can talk to you and explain things to you, but he is never the mind. He comes and stands behind the mind, uses it, just as you drive your car – you never become the car. He uses all these rungs, he is the whole ladder. But his ultimate standpoint remains the transcendental. That is his nature.

Avalokita means one who looks from the beyond at the world.

Avalokita, the holy lord and bodhisattva, was moving in the deep course of the wisdom which has gone beyond. The sutra says this state of beyondness is not a static thing. It is a movement, it is a process, riverlike. It is not a noun, it is a verb. It goes on unfolding. That's why Hindus call it the one-thousand-petaled lotus: "one thousand" simply means infinite, it is symbolic of infinity. Petals upon petals, petals upon petals go on opening, to no end. The journey begins but never ends. It is eternal pilgrimage.

Avalokita, the holy lord and bodhisattva, was moving in the deep course of the wisdom which has gone beyond. He was flowing like a river into the world of the beyond. He is called the holy lord and bodhisattva. Again the Sanskrit word has to be remembered. The Sanskrit word is *iswara*, which is translated as "holy lord." *Iswara* means one who has become absolutely rich from his own riches, whose riches are of his own nature; nobody can take them away, nobody can steal them, they cannot be lost. All the riches that you have can be lost, can be stolen, *will* be lost – one day death will come and will take everything away. When somebody has come to the inner diamond that is his own being, death cannot take it away. Death is irrelevant to it. It cannot be stolen, it cannot be lost. Then one has become *iswara*, then one has become a holy lord. Then one has become *bhagavan*.

The word *bhagavan* simply means "the blessed one." Then one has become the blessed one. Now his blessing is eternally his; it depends on nothing, it is independent. It is not caused by anything so it cannot be taken away. It is uncaused, it is one's intrinsic nature.

And he is called bodhisattva. Bodhisattva is a very beautiful concept in Buddhism. It means one who has become a buddha, but is still holding himself in the world of time and space – to help others. *Bodhisattva* means "essentially a buddha," is just ready to drop and disappear, is ready to go into nirvana. Nothing remains to be solved, all his problems are solved. There is no need for him to be here, but he is still here. There is nothing else to be learned here, but he is still here. And he is keeping himself in body-form, in mind-form – he is keeping the whole ladder. He has gone beyond, but he is keeping the whole ladder – to help, out of compassion.

A story is told that Buddha reached the doors of the ultimate, nirvana. The doors were opened, the angels were dancing and singing to receive him – because it rarely happens that a human being becomes a buddha, in millions of years. The doors open, and that day is naturally a great day of celebration. All the ancient buddhas had gathered, and there was great rejoicing, and flowers were showering, and music was played, and everything was decorated – it was a day of celebration.

But Buddha did not enter the door. The ancient buddhas, all with folded hands, asked him, requested him to come in: "Why are you standing outside?"

And Buddha is reported to have said, "Unless all others who are coming behind me enter, I am not going to enter. I will keep myself outside because once I come in, then I disappear. Then I will not be of any help to these people. I see millions of people stumbling and groping in the dark. I have myself been groping the same way for millions of lives. I would like to give them my hand. Please close the door. When everybody has come, I myself will knock, then you can receive me."

A beautiful story. This is called the state of bodhisattva: one who is ready to disappear but still is holding – in body, in mind, in the world, in time and space – to help others.

Buddha says: "Meditation is enough to solve your problems, but something is missing in it – compassion." If compassion is also there, then you can help others solve their problems. He says: "Meditation is pure gold; it has a perfection of its own. But if there is compassion then the gold has a fragrance too – then a higher perfection, then a new kind of perfection, gold with fragrance." Gold is enough unto itself – very valuable – but with compassion, meditation has a fragrance.

Compassion keeps a buddha remaining a bodhisattva, just on the borderline. Yes, for a few days, a few years, one can hold, but not for long – because by and by things start disappearing on their own. When you are not attached with the body, you become dislocated from there. You can come sometimes, with effort. You can use the body, with effort, but you are no longer settled there. When you are no longer in the mind you can use it sometimes, but it no longer functions as well as it used to function before. You are no longer flowing in it. When you are not using it, it is lying there: it is a mechanism, it starts gathering rust.

When a man has reached the seventh, for a few days, for a few years, he can use the six rungs. He can go back and use them, but by and by they start breaking. By and by, they start dying. A bodhisattva can be here for only one life, at the most. Then he has to disappear because the mechanism disappears.

But all those who have attained have tried, as far as they can, to use the bodymind to help those who are in body and mind, to help those who can understand only the language of the body and the mind, to help the disciples.

Avalokita, the holy lord and bodhisattva, was moving in the deep course of the wisdom which has gone beyond. He looked down from on high, he beheld but five heaps, and he saw that in their own being they were empty. When you look from that point... For example, I was just telling you that I salute the buddha in you. That is one vision from the beyond: that I see you as potential buddhas. And another vision is just that I see you as empty shells.

What you think you are is nothing but an empty shell. Somebody thinks he is a man; that is an empty idea. Consciousness is neither male nor female. Somebody thinks he has a very beautiful body, he is beautiful, strong, this and that – that is an empty idea, just ego deceiving you. Somebody thinks he knows much – that is just meaningless. His mechanism has accumulated memories and he is deceived by the memories. These are all empty things.

So when seeing from the transcendental, on the one side I see you as budding buddhas, on another side I see you just as empty shells.

Buddha has said that man consists of five elements, five *skandhas*, which are all empty. And because of the combination of the five, a by-product arises called the ego, the self. It is just like a clock functioning: it goes on ticking. You can listen and the tick is there; you can open the clock, you can separate all the parts to find where the tick is coming from. Where is the tick? You will not find it anywhere. The tick is a by-product. It is just a combination of a few things. A few things functioning together were creating a tick.

That's what your "I" is – five elements functioning together creating the tick called "I." But it is empty, it has nothing in it. If you go and search for something substantial in it, you will not find anything.

This is one of the Buddha's deepest intuitions, insights: that life is empty, that life as we know it is empty. And life is full too, but we don't know anything about it. From this emptiness you have to move toward a fullness, but that fullness is inconceivable right now – because that fullness from this state will look only empty. From *that* state your fullness looks empty – a king looks like a beggar; a man of knowledge, a knowledgeable man, looks stupid, ignorant.

A small story:

A certain holy man accepted a pupil and said to him, "It would be a good thing if you tried to write down all you understand about the religious life and what has brought you to it."

The pupil went away and began to write. A year later he

came back to the master and said, "I have worked very hard on this, and though it is far from complete, these are the main reasons for my struggle."

The master read the work, which was many thousands of words, and then said to the young man, "It is admirably reasoned and clearly stated, but it is somewhat long. Try to shorten it a little." So the novice went away and after five years he came back with a mere hundred pages.

The master smiled, and after he had read it he said, "Now you are truly approaching the heart of the matter. Your thoughts have clarity and strength. But it is still a little long; try to condense it, my son."

The novice went away sadly, for he had labored hard to reach the essence. But after ten years he came back, and bowing low before the master offered him just five pages and said, "This is the kernel of my faith, the core of my life, and I ask your blessings for having brought me to it."

The master read it slowly and carefully: "It is truly marvelous," he said, "in its simplicity and beauty, but it is not yet perfect. Try to reach a final clarification."

And when the master had reached the time appointed and was preparing for his end, his pupil returned to him again, and kneeling before him to receive his blessings handed him a single sheet of paper on which was written nothing.

Then the master placed his hands on the head of his friend and said, "Now… Now you have understood."

From that transcendental vision, what you have is empty. From your vision, your neurotic vision, what I have is empty.

Buddha looks empty – just pure emptiness – to you. Because of your ideas, because of your clinging, because of your possessiveness about things, Buddha looks empty. Buddha is full: you are empty. And his vision is absolute; your vision is very relative.

The sutra says:

Avolokita, the holy lord and bodhisattva, was moving in the deep course of the wisdom which has gone beyond.
He looked down from on high, he beheld but five heaps, and he saw that in their own being they were empty.

Emptiness is the key to Buddhism – *shunyata*. Meditate over these sutras – meditate with love, with sympathy, not with logic and reasoning. If you go to these sutras with logic and reasoning, you will kill their spirit. Don't dissect them. Try to understand them as they are, and don't bring your mind – your mind will be an interference.

If you can look at these sutras without your mind, great clarity is going to happen to you.

CHAPTER 8

Patanjali and the Path of Yoga

Patanjali's skill in expressing the inexpressible is superb. Nobody has ever been able to surpass him. He has mapped the inner world of consciousness as accurately as it is possible; he has almost done an impossible job.

I have heard a story about Ramakrishna...

One day he said to his disciples, "I will tell you everything today and will not keep anything secret."

He described clearly the centers and the corresponding experiences up to the heart and throat, and then pointing to the spot between the eyebrows he said, "The supreme self is directly known and the individual experiences *samadhi* when the mind comes here. There remains then but a thin transparent screen separating the supreme self and the individual self. The *sadhak* then experiences..."

Saying this, the moment he started to describe in detail the realization of supreme self, he was plunged in *samadhi* and became unconscious. When the *samadhi* came to an end and he came back, he tried again to describe it and was again in *samadhi*; again he became unconscious.

After repeated attempts, Ramakrishna broke into tears and told his disciples that it was impossible to speak about it.

But Ramakrishna has tried, has tried in many ways, from different directions, and this always happened, his whole life. Whenever he comes beyond the third-eye center and is coming nearer *sahasrar*, he is so deeply caught hold of by something inner that the very remembrance of it, the very effort to describe it, and he is gone. For hours he will remain unconscious. It's natural because the bliss of *sahasrar* is such, one is almost overpowered by it. The bliss is so oceanic that one is possessed by it and taken over. One is no longer oneself, once you transcend the third eye.

Ramakrishna tried and failed; could not describe it. Many others have not even tried. Lao Tzu for his whole life resisted saying anything about the world of Tao because of this. Nothing can be said about it, and the moment you try to say it, you are plunged into an inner whirlwind, whirlpool. You are lost, drowned. You are bathed in such beauty and beautitude that you cannot utter a single word.

But Patanjali has done the impossible. He has described as exactly as possible each step, each integration, each chakra – its functioning, and how to transcend it, up to *sahasrar*. And he has even indicated beyond. On each chakra, on each wheel of energy, a certain integration happens.

Let me tell you: at the sex center, the first center – the most primitive but the most natural, the one that is available to all – the integration happens between the outer and the inner. Of course it is momentary. A woman meeting a man or a man meeting a woman come for a single moment, a split moment, where the outer and inner meet and mingle and merge into each other. That's the beauty of sex, the orgasm, that two energies, the complementary energies, meet and become one whole. But it is going to be momentary because the meeting is through the most gross element, the body. The body can touch surfaces but it cannot really enter the other. It is like ice cubes. If you put two ice cubes together, they can touch each other, but if they melt and become water, then they meet and mingle with each other. Then they go to the very center. And if the water evaporates, then the meeting becomes very, very deep. Then there is no I, no thou, no inner, no outer.

The first center, the sex center, gives you a certain integration. That's why there is so much hankering for sex. It is natural. It is in itself beneficial and good. But if you stop there, you have stopped in the porch of a palace. The porch is good, it leads you into the palace, but it is not a place to make your abode, it is not a place to stop forever – and the bliss that is waiting for you on higher integrations of other centers will be missed. In comparison to that bliss and happiness and joy, the beauty of sex is nothing, the pleasure of sex is nothing. It simply gives you a momentary glimpse.

The second chakra is the hara. At the hara, life and death meet. If you reach to the second center, you reach to a higher orgasm of integration; life meeting death, sun meeting moon. And the meeting is inner now, so the meeting can be more permanent, more stable, because you are not dependent on anybody else. Now you are meeting your own inner woman or your own inner man.

The third center is the navel. There the positive and the negative meet – the positive electricity and the negative electricity. Their meeting is even higher than life and death because the electric energy, the *prana*, the bioplasma or bioenergy, is deeper than life and death. It exists before life, it exists after death. Life and death exist because of bioenergy. This meeting of bioenergy at the navel, *nabhi*, gives you even a higher experience of being one: integrated, a unity.

Then is the heart: at the heart center, the lower and the higher meet. At the heart center: the *prakriti* and *purusha*, the sexual and the spiritual, the worldly and the other-worldly – or you can call it the meeting of heaven and earth. It is still higher because for the first time something of the beyond dawns – you can see the sun rising at the horizon. You are still rooted in the earth, but your branches are spreading into the sky. You have become a meeting. That's why the heart center gives the highest and the most refined experience ordinarily available – the experience of love. The experience of love is the meeting of earth and heaven; so love is in a way earthly, and in another way heavenly.

If Jesus defined God as love, this is the reason because in human consciousness, love seems to be the higher glimpse.

Ordinarily people never go beyond the heart center. Even to reach to the heart center seems to be difficult, almost impossible. People remain at the sex center. If they are trained deeply in yoga, karate, aikido, tai chi, then they reach to the second center, the hara. If they are trained in a deep mechanism of breathing, *prana*, then they reach the navel center. And if they are trained how to look beyond earth and how to see beyond the body and how to look so deeply and so sensitively that you are no longer confined to the gross, and the subtle can penetrate its first rays into you – only then, the heart.

All paths of devotion – bhakti yoga – work on the heart center. Tantra starts from the sex center, Tao starts from the hara center. Yoga starts from the navel center. Bhakti yoga, paths of devotion and love, Sufis and others, start from the heart center.

Higher than the heart is the throat center. Again there happens another integration, even more superior, more subtle. This center is the center of receiving and giving. When the child is born he receives from the throat center. First, life enters him from the throat center – he sucks air, breathes; and then he sucks milk from his mother. The child functions from the throat center, but it is half functioning and soon he forgets about it. He just receives, he cannot give yet; his love is passive. And if you are asking for love, then you remain juvenile, you remain childish. Unless you mature – so that you can give love – you have not become a grown-up. Everybody asks for love, demands love, and almost nobody gives. That's the misery all over the world. And everybody who demands thinks that he is giving, believes that he is giving.

I have looked into thousands of people – all hungry for love, thirsty for love, but nobody in any way trying to give. And they all believe that they are giving but not receiving. Once you give you naturally receive. It has never happened otherwise. The moment you give, love rushes into you. It has nothing to do with people; it has something to do with the cosmic energy of existence.

The throat center is the meeting of receiving and giving. You receive from it and you give from it. That is the meaning of Christ's saying that unless you become a child again…. If you translate it into the yoga terminology it will mean: unless you come to the throat center again… The child forgets by and by.

If you look into Freudian psychology, you will have a parallel. Freud says the first stage of the child is oral, the second stage is anal, and the third stage is genital. The whole of Freudian psychology ends with the third. Of course it is a very poor psychology, very rudimentary, fragmentary, and concerned with the very lower functioning of human beings. Oral – yes, the child uses the throat center, just to receive. And once he has started receiving, his being moves to the anal.

Have you seen that a few people cling to the oral, even up to their death? These are the people you will find smoking; these are oral people. They still go on… The smoke, the cigarette, the cigar, gives them a feeling as if something hot like mother's milk is passing through the throat center; they remain confined to the oral and they cannot give. If a person is a chain-smoker, heavy smoker, almost always he is not a giver of love. He demands, but he will not give.

People who are smoking too much are always interested in women's breasts – bound to be because a cigarette is a substitute for the nipple. I am not saying that people who are not smokers are not interested in women's breasts. Those who smoke are interested; those who don't smoke are also interested – they may be chewing pan or gum or something else, or they may be simply interested in pornography, or they may be just obsessed by the breast continuously. In their mind, in their dream, in their imagination, fantasy, the breast – breasts and breasts go on floating all around them. These are oral people, stuck.

When Jesus says you have to be a child again, he means you have to come back to the throat center, but with a new energy to give. All creative people are givers. They may sing a song for you or dance a dance or write a poem or paint a picture or tell you a story. For all these, the throat center is again used as a center to give. The meeting of receiving and giving happens at the throat. The capacity to receive and to give is one of the greatest integrations.

There are people who are only capable of receiving. They will remain miserable because you never become rich by receiving. You become rich by giving. In fact, you possess only that which you can give. If you cannot give it, you simply believe that you possess. You don't possess it; you are not a master. If you cannot give your money, then you are not the master of it. Then money is the master. If you can give it, then certainly you are the master. This will look like a paradox, but let me repeat it: you are the possessor only of that which you give. The moment you give, in that very moment you have become a possessor, enriched; giving enriches you.

Miserly people are the most miserable and poor people in the world – poorer than the poor. They cannot give: they are stuck. They go on hoarding. Their hoarding becomes a burden on their being – it does not free them. In fact, if you have something you will become freer. But look at the misers. They have much, but they are burdened; they are not free. Even beggars are freer than they. What has happened to them? They have used their throat center just to receive. Not only have they not used their throat center to give, they have not even moved to the second Freudian center, anal. These people are always constipated; hoarders, misers, always suffer from constipation. Remember, I am not saying that all people who have constipation are misers; there may be other reasons. But misers are certainly constipated.

Freud says that there is something in gold and excreta. Both look yellow, and people who are constipatory are too attracted to gold. Otherwise gold has no existential value – some psychological value, but no existential value. You cannot eat it, you cannot drink it. What can you do with it? Even a glass of water is more valuable existentially. But why has gold become so valuable? Why are people so obsessed with gold? They have not moved from the oral to the anal. They are constipated in their inner being. Now their whole life will reflect their constipation: they will become hoarders of gold. Gold is symbolic. The yellowness gives them some idea.

Have you watched small children? It is difficult to persuade them to go to the toilet, they have almost to be forced to go to the toilet. And even then they insist, "Nothing is happening. Can I come back?" They are learning the first lessons of miserliness – how to hold on. How to hold on, how not to give even that which is useless, even that which is harmful if you keep it within you. Even poison – it is difficult for them to leave it, to renounce it.

I have heard about two Buddhist *bhikkhus*…

One of them was a miser and a hoarder and he used to collect money and keep it, and the other used to laugh at this foolish attitude. Whatsoever will come on his way, he will use it, he will never hoard it. One night they came across a river. It was evening; the sun was setting and it was dangerous to stay there. They had to go to the other shore. There was a town; this side was simply wilderness.

The hoarder said, "Now you don't have any money, so we cannot pay the ferryman? What do you say now about it? You are against hoarding. Now if I don't have any money we both will die. You see the point?" He said, "Money is needed."

The man who believed in renunciation laughed, but he didn't say anything. Then the hoarder paid and they crossed the river; they reached the other shore.

The hoarder again said, "Now remember, next time don't start arguing with me. You see? Money helps. Without money we would have been dead. The whole night on the other shore, it was dangerous to survive – wild animals."

The other *bhikkhu* laughed and he said, "But we have come across the river because you could renounce it. It is not because of hoarding that we have survived. If you had insisted on hoarding it and you were not going to pay the ferryman, we would have died. It is because you could renounce – because you could leave it, you could give it – that's why we have survived."

The argument must be continuing still. But remember, I am not against money. I am all for it, but use it! Possess it, own it; but your ownership arises only the moment you have become capable of giving it. At the throat center this new synthesis happens. You can accept and you can give.

There are people who change from one extreme to another. First they were incapable of giving, they could only receive; then they change, they go to the other extreme – now they can give but they cannot receive. That too is lopsidedness. A real man is capable of accepting gifts and giving them back. In India you will find many sannyasins, many so-called mahatmas, who will not touch money. If you give them any, they will shrink back, as if you have produced a snake or something poisonous. Their shrinking back shows that now they have moved to the other extreme: now they have become incapable of receiving. Again their throat center is half-functioning, and a center never functions really unless it functions fully – unless the wheel moves all the way, goes on moving and creates energy fields.

Then is the third-eye center: At the third-eye center the right and left meet, *pingala* and *ida* meet, and become *sushumna*. The two hemispheres of the brain meet at the third eye: that is just between the two eyes. One eye represents the right, another eye represents the left, and it is just in the middle. The left and right brains meeting at the third eye is a very high synthesis. People have been capable of describing up to this point. That's why Ramakrishna could describe up to the third eye. And when he started to talk about the final, the ultimate synthesis that happens at *sahasrar*, he again and again fell into silence, into *samadhi*. He was drowned in it; it was too much. It was floodlike; he was taken over to the ocean. He could not keep himself conscious, alert.

The ultimate synthesis happens at *sahasrar*, the crown chakra. Because of this *sahasrar*, all over the world kings, emperors, monarchs, and queens, use the crown. It has become formal, but basically it was accepted because unless your *sahasrar* is functioning, how can you be a monarch, how can you be a king? How can you rule people if you have not even become a ruler of yourself? In the symbol of the crown a secret is hidden. The secret is that a person who has reached to the crown center, the ultimate synthesis of his being – only he should be the king or the queen, nobody else. Only he is capable of ruling others, because he has come to rule himself. He has become a master of himself; now he can be helpful to others also.

Really, when you achieve to *sahasrar*, a crown flowers within you, a one-thousand-petaled lotus opens. No crown can be compared with it, but then it became just a symbol and the symbol has existed all over the world. That simply shows that everywhere people became alert and aware in one way or other of the ultimate synthesis in the *sahasrar*. Jews use the skullcap – it is exactly on the *sahasrar*. Hindus allow a bunch of hair, they call it *choti*, the peak, to grow exactly on the spot where the *sahasrar* is, or has to be. There are a few Christian societies which shave just that part of the head. When a master blesses a disciple, he puts his hand on the *sahasrar*. And if the disciple is really receptive, surrendered, he will suddenly feel an upsurge of energy, running from the sex center to the *sahasrar*.

Sometimes when I touch your head and you suddenly become sexual don't be afraid, don't shrink back, because that is how it should be. The energy is at the sex center. It starts uncoiling itself. You become afraid, you shrink, you repress it – what is happening? And becoming sexual at the feet of your master seems to be a little awkward, embarrassing. It is not. Allow it, let it be, and soon you will see it has passed the first center and the second and, if you are surrendered, within a second the energy is moving at the *sahasrar* and you will have a feeling of a new opening within you. That's why a disciple is supposed to bow his head, so the master can touch the head.

The last synthesis is of object and subject, the outer and inner, again. In a sexual orgasm outer and inner meet, but momentarily. In *sahasrar* they meet permanently. That's why I say one has to travel from sex to *samadhi*. In sex, ninety-nine percent is sex, one percent is *sahasrar*; in *sahasrar*, ninety-nine percent is *sahasrar*, one percent is sex. The two are joined, they are bridged, by deep currents of energy. So if you have enjoyed sex, don't make your abode there. Sex is just a glimpse of *sahasrar*. *Sahasrar* is going to deliver a thousandfold, a millionfold, a bliss to you, benediction to you.

The outer and the inner meet, "I" and "thou" meet, man and woman meet, yin and yang meet; and the meeting is absolute. Then there is no parting, then there is no divorce.

This is called yoga. *Yoga* means the meeting of the two into one. In Christianity, mystics have called it *unio mystica*. That is the exact translation of *yoga* – *unio mystica*: the mysterious union. At the *sahasrar* the alpha and the omega meet, the beginning and the end. The beginning is in the sex center, sex is your alpha; *samadhi* is your omega. And unless alpha and omega meet, unless you have attained to this supreme union, you will remain miserable because your destiny is that. You will remain unfulfilled. You can be fulfilled only at this highest peak of synthesis.

Now the sutras.

Performing samyama on their power of cognition,
real nature, egoism, all pervasiveness, and functions
brings mastery over the sense organs.

The first thing to be understood is that you have senses but you have lost sensitivity. Your senses are almost dull, dead. They are there hanging with you, but energy is not flowing in them; they are not alive limbs of your being. Something has deadened within you, has become cold, blocked. It has happened to the whole of humanity because of thousands of years of repression. And thousands of years of conditioning and ideologies which are against the body have crippled you. You live only for name's sake.

So the first thing to be done is: your senses should become really alive and sensitive. Only then can they be mastered. You see but you don't see deeply. You see only the surface of things. You touch but your touch has no warmth; nothing flows in and out from your touch. You hear also. The birds go on singing and you hear and you can say, "Yes, I am hearing," and you are not wrong – you are hearing, but it never reaches to the very core of your being. It does not go dancing within you; it doesn't help a flowering, an unfolding within you.

These senses have to be rejuvenated. Yoga is not against the body, remember. Yoga says go beyond the body, but it is not against the body. Yoga says use the body, don't be used by it; but it is not against the body. Yoga says the body is your temple. You are in the body, and the body is so beautiful an organism, so complex and so subtle, so mysterious, and so many dimensions open through it. And those are the only doors and windows you will reach to existence through. So don't deaden them; make them more alive. Let them vibrate, pulsate, and, what Stanley Keleman has said: "Let them 'stream.'" That is exactly the right word: let them flow like a stream, rushing. You can have the sensation. Your hand, if it is rushing like a stream of energy: you will feel a tingling sensation, you will feel something inside the hand is flowing and wants to make contact, wants to be connected.

When you love a woman or a man and you take her hand in your hand, if your hand is not streaming, this love is not going to be of any use. If your hand is not jumping and throbbing with energy and pouring energy into your woman or into your man, then this love is almost dead from the very beginning. Then this child is not born alive. Then sooner or later you will be finished – you are already finished. It will take a little time to recognize because your mind is also dull; otherwise you would not enter it because it is already dead. For what are you entering? You take time to recognize things because your sensitivity, brilliance, intelligence, is so clouded and confused.

Only a streaming love can become a source of blissfulness, of joy, of delight. But for that you will need your senses streaming.

Sometimes you have that glimpse also; and everybody had it when he was a child. Watch a child running after a butterfly. He is streaming, as if any moment he can jump out of his body. Watch a child when he is looking at a roseflower. See his eyes, the brilliance, the light that comes to his eyes. He is streaming. His eyes are almost dancing on the petals of the flower.

This is the way to be: be riverlike. And only then is it possible to master these senses. In fact, people have had a very wrong attitude. They think that if you want to master your senses, you have to make them almost dead. But then what is the point of mastering? You can kill, and you are the master. You can sit on the corpse. But what is the point of being a master? But this looked easier: first kill them and then you can master. If the body feels too strong, fast. Make it weak, and then you start feeling that you are the master – but you have killed the body. Remember, life has to be mastered, not dead things. They will not be of any use.

But this has been found to be a shortcut, so all the religions of the world have been using it. Destroy your body by and by. Disconnect yourself from the body. Don't be in contact, remove yourself, become indifferent. When your body is almost a dead tree – no longer do leaves come to it, no longer does it flower, no longer do birds come to rest. It is just a dead stump. Of course you can master it, but now what are you going to gain from this mastery?

This is the problem; that's why people don't understand what Patanjali means.

Performing samyama *on their power of cognition…* Your eyes see, your ears hear, your nose smells, your tongue tastes, your hands make contact, your feet make connectedness with the earth – that is their power of cognition.

Performing samyama *on their power of cognition…* But they have to be powerful. Otherwise you will not be able to even feel what power is. These senses have to be so full of power, so high with power, that you can perform *samyama*, that you can meditate upon them.

Right now when you look at a flower, the flower is there, but have you ever felt your eyes? You see the flower, but have you felt the power of your eyes? It should be there because you are using your eyes to see the flower. And of course, eyes are more beautiful than any flower because all flowers have to come through the eyes. It is through the eyes that you have become aware of the world of flowers, but have you ever felt the power of the eyes? They are almost dull, dead. They have become passive, just like windows, receptive. They don't go to their object.

And power means being active. Power means your eyes going and almost touching the flower, your ears going and almost touching the songs of the birds, your hands going with the total energy in you, focused there and touching your beloved. Or you are lying down on the grass, and your whole body, full of power, meeting in a contact with the grass, having a dialogue with the grass. Or you are swimming in the river and whispering with the river and listening to the whispers of the river – connected, in communion – but power is needed.

So the first thing I would like you to do is when you see, really see, become the eyes. Forget everything. Let your whole energy flow through the eyes. Your eyes will be cleaned, bathed in an inner shower, and you will be able to see that these trees are no longer the same, the greenery is no longer the same. It has become greener, as if dust has disappeared from it. The dust was not on the trees, it was on your eyes. And you will see for the first time and you will hear for the first time.

Jesus goes on saying to his disciples, "If you have ears listen. If you have eyes see." They were not all blind, and they were not all deaf. What does he mean? He means that you have almost become deaf and almost become blind. You see and yet you don't see. You hear yet you don't hear. It is not a power, it is not energy, it is not vital.

Performing samyana *on their power of cognition, real nature…* Then you will be able to see what is the real nature of your senses. It is divine. Your body embodies the divine. It is the divine who has looked through your eyes.

I remember Meister Eckhart's famous saying. The day he realized and became enlightened, his friends and disciples and brothers asked, "What have you seen?" He laughed. He is the only one in the whole of Christianity who comes very close to Zen masters, almost a Zen master. He laughed. He said, "I have not seen the divine. It has seen itself through me. The divine has seen itself through me. These eyes are the divine's. And what a game, what a play. It has seen itself through me."

When you really feel the nature of your senses, you will feel it is divine. It is existence who has moved through your hand. It is existence's hand. All hands are its. It is existence who has loved through you. All love affairs are existence's. And how can it be otherwise? Hindus call it *leela* – a play. It is existence who is calling you through the cuckoo, and it is existence who is listening through you. It is it and it alone spread all over.

Performing samyama on their power of cognition, real nature, egoism, all-pervasiveness, and functions brings mastery over the sense organs. This word egoism has to be understood because in Sanskrit we have three words for the ego and in English there is only one word. That creates difficulty. The Sanskrit word in the sutra is asmita, so let me first explain it to you.

There are three words: *ahankar, asmita, atma*. All mean *I*. *Ahankar* can be translated as the *ego* – the very gross, too much emphasis on "I." For *asmita* there is no word in English. *Asmita* means amness. I am; in ego the emphasis is on "I"; in *asmita* the emphasis is on "am." Amness, purer than ego. Still it is there, but in a very different form. Amness. And *atma*: even amness has disappeared. In the ego "I am"; in *asmita* only "am"; in *atma* even that has disappeared. In *atma* there is pure being, neither I nor amness.

In this sutra, *asmita* is used, amness. Remember, the ego is of the mind; senses have no ego. They have a certain amness but no ego. The ego is of the mind. Your eyes don't have any ego; your hands don't have any ego. They have a certain amness. That's why if your skin has to be replaced and somebody else's skin is planted on you, your body will reject it because the body knows "it is not mine." So your own skin has to be replaced from some other part of the body, from your thighs. Your own skin has to be replaced, otherwise the body will reject. The body will not accept it: "It is not mine." The body has no I but it has an amness.

If you need blood, anybody's blood won't do. The body will not accept all sorts of blood, only a particular blood. It has its own amness. That will be accepted; some other blood will be rejected. The body has its own feel of its being – *very* unconscious, *very* subtle and pure, but it is there.

Your eyes are yours, just like your thumbprints. Everything yours is yours. Now physiologists say that everybody's heart is different, of a different shape. In physiology books, the picture that you will find is not a real picture. It is just average. It is just imagined. Otherwise each person's heart has a different shape. Even each person's kidney has a different shape. These parts all have their signatures; everybody is so unique. That is the amness.

You will never be here again, you have never been before, so move cautiously and alertly and happily. Just think: the glory of your being. Just think: that you are so superb and unique. Existence has vested much in you – never imitate because that will be a betrayal. Be yourself. Let that be your religion. All else is politics. Don't be a Hindu, don't be a Mohammedan, don't be a Christian. Be religious, but there is only one religion, and that is just being yourself, authentically yourself.

Performing samyama on their power of cognition, real nature, – asmita, the subtle amness – all-pervasiveness, and functions brings mastery over the sense organs. And if you meditate on these things, you will become a master. Meditation brings mastery; nothing else brings mastery except meditation. If you meditate on your eye, first you will see the roseflower; by and by you will be able to see the eye that is seeing. Then you have become a master of the eye. Once you have seen the seeing eye, you have become a master. Now you can use all its energies; and they are all-pervasive. Your eyes are not as limited as you think them to be. They can see many more things which you have not seen. They can penetrate many more mysteries that you have not even dreamed about. But you are not master of your eyes, and you have used them in a very haphazard way, not knowing what you are doing.

And in contact so much with objects, you have forgotten the subjectivity of your eyes. It happens if you keep company with someone – by and by you become influenced by him. You have been in contact with objects too much and you have forgotten the inner quality of your senses. You see things, but you never see your seeing. You hear the songs, but you never hear the subtle vibration that goes on within you, the sound of your being.

Let me tell you an anecdote...

I have heard that an extremely confident tramp had enormous nerve. He had just completed a very large meal in a swanky restaurant when he announced to the manager, "My good man, I have really enjoyed your food, but unfortunately I cannot afford to pay for any of it at all. I have not a penny to my name.

"Now don't get angry. I am by profession a beggar, as you may see. I happen to be an extremely talented beggar too. I can go out and within one hour get the money I owe you for this meal. Naturally though, you cannot trust me to come back, and this I fully understand. You would be most welcome to accompany me, but can a man like you, a well-known restaurant owner, afford to be seen with a man of my caliber? No. So I have, sir, the perfect solution to our little problem. I will wait here and you go out and beg until you have the cost of this meal."

If you keep company with a beggar, you will become a beggar. He will suggest in a thousand and one ways to you to become like him.

We have kept company with objects so long that we have forgotten our subjectivity. We have remained focused outwardly so long on things that we have forgotten that we are persons. This long association with objects has completely destroyed your image of yourself. You have to come back home.

In yoga, when you start seeing your seeing eye, you come across a subtle energy. They call it *tanmatra*. When you can see your eye seeing, just hidden behind the eyes you see a tremendous energy – that is *tanmatra*, the energy of the eye. Behind the ear you see tremendous energy accumulated, *tanmatra* of the ear. Behind your genital organs you see tremendous energy accumulated, *tanmatra* of sexuality. And so on, so forth. Everywhere behind your senses there is a pool of energy, unused. Once you know it, you can pour that energy into your eyes, and then you will see visions which only sometimes poets see, painters see. Then you will hear sounds which only sometimes musicians hear, poets hear. And then you will touch things which only sometimes in rare moments lovers know how to touch.

You will become alive, streaming.

Ordinarily you have been taught to repress your senses, not to know them. It is very foolish, but very convenient.

It happened…

After a rural wedding, the bride and the groom climbed into the wagon and set out for their farm home. About a mile down the road, the horse stumbled. "That's one!" shouted the groom.

They continued on and the horse stumbled again. "That is two!" shouted the groom.

As they neared the farm, the horse stumbled again. "That is three!" shouted the groom and, seizing a gun from behind the seat, put a bullet through the horse's brain.

The bride sat aghast. Then, in no uncertain terms, she told her new husband what she thought of his action. He sat quietly until she subsided, then pointed at her and shouted, "That is one!"

The couple lived happily for sixty years.

But that happiness cannot be real happiness. Easy to repress at the point of a gun, but then what sort of love will happen between these two people? The gun will always stand in between, and the wife will always be afraid that now any moment he is going to say, "Now this is two! Now this is three!" and finished!

That's what you have done with your senses, with your body – you have repressed it. But you were helpless. I don't say that you are responsible for repressing it. You were brought up in such a way, nobody allowed your senses freedom. In the name of love, only repression continues. The mothers, the fathers, the society, they go on repressing. By and by they teach you a trick, and the trick is not to accept yourself, deny. Everything has to be channeled into conformity. Your wilderness has to be thrown into the dark part of your soul and a small corner has to be clean, like a drawing room, where you can see people, meet people, and live and forget all about your wilder being: your real existence. Your fathers and your mothers are not responsible either because they were brought up in the same way.

So nobody is responsible. But once you know it, and you don't do anything, *then* you become responsible. Being near me I am going to make you very, very responsible because you will know it, and then if you don't do anything, then you cannot throw the responsibility on anybody else. Then you are going to be responsible!

Now you know about how you have destroyed your senses, and you know also how to revive them. Do something. Throw the gun away completely, the repressive mind completely. Unblock yourself. Start flowing again, start connecting again with your being, start connecting with your senses again. You are like a disconnected telephone line. Everything looks perfectly okay, the telephone is there but the line is disconnected. Your eyes are there, your hands are there, your ears are there, but the line is disconnected. Reconnect it. If it can be disconnected, it can be reconnected. Others have disconnected it because they were also taught in the same way, but you can reconnect it.

All my meditations are to give you a streaming energy. That's why I call them dynamic methods. Old meditations were just to sit silently, not to do anything. I give you active methods because when you are streaming with energy you can sit silently, that will do, but right now first you have to become alive.

From this follows instantaneous cognition
without the use of the body,

*and complete mastery over pradhana, prakriti, the material
world.*

If you can see *tanmatras*, the subtle energies of your senses,
you will become capable of using your cognition without the
grosser instruments. If you know that behind the eye there is an
accumulated pool of energy, you can close your eyes and use that
energy directly. Then you will be able to see without opening
your eyes. That's what telepathy, clairvoyance, clairaudience is.

In Russia, there is a woman who has been investigated scien-
tifically who stands just twenty feet away from any object and
starts pulling it, just by energy. She makes movements with her
hands, twenty feet away, as you have seen a hypnotist making
passes, she simply draws, gestures. Within fifteen minutes, things
start moving toward her. She has not touched them. Much inves-
tigation has been done about what happens. And that woman
loses at least half a pound in weight in a half-hour experiment.
Certainly she is losing some sort of energy.

This is what yoga calls *tanmatra*. Ordinarily you use the
energy through the hand, when you pick something up: a stone,
a rock. You carry it; you use the same energy through the hand.
But if you know the energy directly, you can drop the use of the
hand. The energy can move the object directly. In the same way
– telepathy: you can hear or read people's thoughts or can see
faraway scenes. Once you know the *tanmatra*, the subtle energy
that is being used by your eyes, the eyes can be discarded. Once
you know that it is not really the sense that is functioning but
the energy, you are freed of the sense.

I have heard a story...

So this guy phoned Cohen & Goldberg, wholesalers.
"Put me through to Mr. Cohen, please."
"I am afraid Mr. Cohen has gone out, sir," said the switch-
board girl.

"Then get me Mr. Goldberg."

"I am afraid Mr. Goldberg is tied up at present, sir."

"Okay, I will phone back later."

Ten minutes later: "Mr. Goldberg, please."

"I am afraid Mr. Goldberg is still tied up, sir."

"I will phone back."

Half an hour later: "Get me Mr. Goldberg."

"I am terribly sorry, sir, but Mr. Goldberg is still tied up."

"I will phone back."

Another half an hour later: "Goldberg!"

"I have dreadful news for you, sir. Mr. Goldberg is still tied up."

"But look, this is ridiculous. How can you run a business like that? One partner is out all morning and the other is tied up for hours on end. What is going on there?"

"Well, you see, sir, whenever Mr. Cohen goes out, he ties up Mr. Goldberg."

This is what is happening inside you also. Whenever you go out, through the eyes, through the hands, through your genital organs, through your ears – whenever you go out, continuously a certain type of bondage and tying is created. By and by you become tight with the particular sense – eyes, ears – because that is from where you go out, again, again, again. By and by you forget the energy that is going out.

This getting into bondage with the senses is the whole world, the samsara. How to untie yourself from the senses? And once you are tied up with the senses, you start thinking in terms of them. You forget yourself.

Another story…

A disciple wanted very much to renounce the world and follow his guru, but he said that his wife and family loved him too much and he was unable to leave his home.

The guru came up with a plan. The man was taught certain yogic secrets so that he could give the appearance to all who looked upon his body that he was deceased. The next day the man followed instructions and his body was besieged with the wailings and sobbings of his wife and family.

The guru appeared at the door in the guise of a magician and told the family that if they loved this man so much, he could bring him back to life. He said that the man would live if someone would die in his place by drinking the potion he had.

Each member of the family had an excuse that made it necessary to keep his own life, and the wife added, "Anyway, he is already dead; we will manage."

At this the yogi stood up and said, "Woman, if you can live without me, then I can go with my guru." He faced the teacher and said, "Let us go, sir, Revered Master. I will follow you."

The whole attachment to the senses is as if you *are* the senses, as if you cannot live without them, as if your whole life is confined to them. But you are not confined to them. You can renounce them, and you can still live, and live on a higher plane. Difficult! Just as if you want to persuade a seed, "Die, and soon a beautiful plant will be born." How can he believe, because he will be dead? No seed has ever known that by his death a new sprout comes up, a new life arises. So how to believe it? Or if you go near an egg and you want to persuade the bird within, "Come out," but how is the bird to believe that there is any possibility of life without the egg? Or if you talk to a child inside the womb of a mother and tell him, "Come out, don't be afraid," but he knows nothing outside the womb. The womb has been his whole life; he knows only that. He is afraid. The same is the situation: surrounded by the senses, we live in a sort of confinement, an imprisonment.

One has to be a little daring, courageous. Right now, wherever you are and whatsoever you are, nothing is happening to you. Then take the risk. Then move into the unknown. Then try to find a new way of life.

From this follows instantaneous cognition without the use of the body, and complete mastery over prakriti, *the material world.* Up to now you have been possessed by the material world. Once you know that you have your own energy, totally independent from the material world, you become a master. No longer does world possess you; you possess it. Only those who renounce become the real masters.

> *Only after the awareness of the distinction*
> *between sattva and purusha*
> *does supremacy and knowledge arise*
> *over all states of existence.*

And the subtlest discrimination has to be made between *sattva* and *purusha* – intelligence and awareness. It is very easy to separate yourself from the body. The body is so gross you can feel it, you cannot be it. You must be inside it. It is easy to see that you cannot be the eyes. You must be someone hidden behind who looks through the eyes; otherwise who will look through the eyes? Your glasses cannot look. Behind the glasses, eyes are needed. Your eyes are also like glasses. They *are* glasses; they cannot look. You are needed somewhere behind to look.

But the subtlest identification is with intelligence. Your power to think, your power of intellect, understanding, is the subtlest thing. It is very difficult to discriminate between awareness and intelligence. But it can be discriminated.

By and by, step-by-step, first, know that you are not the body. Let that understanding grow deep, crystallize. Then know that you are not the senses. Let that understanding grow, crystallize. Then know that you are not the *tanmatras*, the energy pools behind the senses. Let that grow and crystallize. And then you will be able to see that intelligence is also a pool of energy. It is the common pool, in which eyes pour their energy, ears pour their energy, hands pour their energy. All the senses are like rivers and intelligence is the central thing, in which they bring information and pour.

Whatever your mind knows is given by the senses. You have seen colors: your mind knows them. If you are color-blind, if you cannot see the color green, then your mind does not know anything about green.

Bernard Shaw lived his whole life unaware that he was color-blind. It is very difficult to come to know it, but one accidental incident allowed him to become aware. On one of his birthdays somebody presented him a suit, but the tie was missing, so he went to the market to find a tie which could fit with the suit. The suit was green, and he started purchasing a yellow tie. His secretary was watching, and she asked, "What are you doing? It won't fit. The suit is green and the tie is yellow."

He said, "Is there a difference between these two?"

For seventy years he had lived not knowing that he could not see yellow. He saw green. Whether it was yellow or green, both colors looked green. Yellow was not part of his mind; the eyes never poured that information into the mind.

The eyes are like servants, information collectors, public relations officers, roaming all over the world, collecting things, pouring into the mind. They go on feeding the mind; the mind is the central pool.

First you have to become aware that you are not the eye, not the energy that is hidden behind the eye, then you will be able to see that every sense is pouring into the mind. You are not this mind, also. You are the one who is seeing it being poured. You are just standing on the bank, all the rivers pouring into the ocean – you are the watcher, the witness.

Swami Ram has said: "Science is difficult to define, but

perhaps the most essential feature of it involves the study of something which is external to the observer. The techniques of meditation offer an approach which allows one to be external to one's own internal states."

"The techniques of meditation offer an approach which allows one to be external to one's own internal states" – and the ultimate of meditation is to know that whatever you can know, you are not it. Whatever can be reduced to a known object, you are not it, because you cannot be reduced to an object. You remain eternally subject – the knower, the knower, the knower. And the knower can never be reduced to the known.

This is *purusha*, awareness. This is the final understanding that arises out of yoga. Meditate over it.

CHAPTER 9

The Subtle Bodies According to Patanjali

The yoga system of Patanjali is not a philosophical system. It is empirical; it is a tool to work with – but still it has a philosophy. That too, is just to give an intellectual understanding of where you are moving, what you are seeking. But philosophy is arbitrary, utilitarian, just to give a comprehensive picture of the territory you are going to discover; but the philosophy has to be understood.

The first thing about Patanjali's philosophy is that he divides human personality into five seeds, five bodies. He says you don't have one body; you have layers upon layers of bodies – five layers.

The first body he calls *annamay kosh* – the food body, the earth body, which is made of earth and is constantly to be nourished by food. Food comes from the earth. If you stop taking food, your *annamay kosh* will wither away. So one has to be very alert to what one is eating because that makes you and it will affect you in millions of ways. Sooner or later your food is not just food – it becomes blood, your bones, your very marrow. It circulates in your being and goes on affecting you. So the purity of food creates a pure *annamay kosh* – the pure food body.

And if the first body is pure, light, not heavy, then it is easy to enter the second body; otherwise it will be difficult, you will be loaded. Have you seen that when you have eaten too much, and heavy foods…? Immediately you start feeling a sort of sleep, a sort of lethargy. You would like to go to sleep; awareness immediately starts disappearing. When the first body is loaded it is difficult to create great awareness. Hence fasting became so important in all the religions. But fasting is a science and one should not fool around with it.

Just the other night a sannyasin came and she told me that she has been fasting and now her whole body, her whole being, is disturbed – tremendously disturbed. Now the stomach is not functioning well, and when the stomach is not functioning well, everything is weakened, the vitality is lost, and you cannot be alive. You become more and more insensitive and dead.

But fasting is important. It should be done very carefully; one should understand the functioning of the *annamay kosh* – only then. And it should be done under the proper guidance of one who has moved through all the phases of his *annamay kosh*. Not only that, one who has gone beyond it and who can look at the *annamay kosh* as a witness; otherwise fasting can be dangerous. Then, just the right amount of food and the right quality of food has to be practiced; fasting is not needed.

But this is important because this is your first body and, more or less, people cling to their first body; they never move to the second. Millions of people are not even aware that they have a second body, a deeper body, hidden behind the first sheath. The first covering is very gross.

The second body Patanjali calls *pranamay kosh* – the energy body, electric body. The second consists of electric fields. That's what acupuncture is all about. This second body is more subtle than the first, and people who start moving from the first body to the second become fields of energy, tremendously attractive, magnetic, hypnotic. If you go near them, you will feel vitalized, charged.

If you go near a man who lives only in his food body, you will be depleted – he will suck you. Many times you come across people and you feel that they suck you. After they have left, you feel depleted, dissipated, as if somebody has exploited your energy. The first body is a sucker, and the first body is very gross. So if you live too much with first body-oriented people, you will feel always burdened, tense, bored, sleepy, with no energy, always at the point of the lowest rung of your energy; and you will not have any energy which can be used for higher growth.

This type, the first type, the *annamay-kosh* oriented person lives for food. He eats and eats and eats, and that's his whole life. He remains in a way childish. The first thing that the child does in the world is to suck air, and then to suck milk. The first thing the child has to do in the world is to help the food body, and if a person remains food addicted, he remains childish; his growth suffers.

The second body, *pranamay kosh*, gives you a new freedom, gives you more space. The second body is bigger than the first; it is not confined to your physical body. It is inside the physical body and it is outside the physical body; it surrounds you like a subtle climate, an aura of energy. Now in Russia they have discovered that photographs can be taken of this energy body. They call it "bioplasma," but it exactly means *prana* – the energy, elan vital, or what Taoists call chi. It can be photographed; now it has become almost scientific.

A very great discovery has been done in Russia, and that is that before your physical body suffers an illness the energy body suffers it – six months before – then it happens to the physical body. If you are going to have tuberculosis, or cancer, or any illness, your energy body starts showing indications of it six months before. No examination, no testing of the physical body shows anything, but the electric body starts showing it. First it appears in the *pranamay kosh*, then it enters the *annamay kosh*.

So now they say that it has become possible to treat a person before he has fallen ill. Once it becomes so, then there is no need for humanity to fall ill. Before you become aware that you are ill, your photographs by Kirlian methods will show that some illness is going to happen to your physical body; it can be prevented in the *pranamay kosh*.

That's why yoga insists so much on the purity of breathing, because the *pranamay kosh* is made of a subtle energy that travels with the breathing, inside you. If you breathe rightly, your *pranamay kosh* remains healthy and whole and alive. Such a person never feels tired; such a person is always available to do anything. Such a person is always responsive, always ready to respond to the moment, ready to take the challenge. He is always ready. You will never find him unprepared for any moment. Not that he plans for the future, no – but he has so much energy that whatsoever happens he is ready to respond. He has overflowing energy. Tai chi works on *pranamay kosh*. *Pranayam* works on *pranamay kosh*.

If you know just how to breathe naturally, you will grow into your second body. And the second body is stronger than the first. And the second body lives longer than the first.

When somebody dies, for almost three days you can see his bioplasma. Sometimes that is mistaken for his ghost. The physical body dies, but the energy body continues to move. And those who have experimented deeply about death say that for three days it is very difficult for the person who has died to believe that he has died, because the same form – and more vital than ever, more healthy than ever, more beautiful than ever – surrounds him. It depends on how big a bioplasma you have; then it can continue for thirteen days or even for more.

Around the *samadhis* of yogis – in India we burn everybody's body except the body of one who has attained to *Samadhi*; we don't burn his body for a certain reason. Once you burn the body, the bioplasma starts moving away from the earth. You can feel it for a few days, but then it disappears into the cosmos. But if the physical body is left, then the bioplasma can cling to it. And a man who has attained *samadhi*, who has become enlightened, if his bioplasma can remain somewhere around his *samadhi*, many people will be benefited by it. That's how many people come to see their gurus' forms.

In the Aurobindo ashram, Aurobindo's body is put in a *samadhi*, not destroyed, not burned. Many people have felt as if they have seen Aurobindo around it. Or sometimes they have heard the same footsteps, the way Aurobindo used to walk, and sometimes he is there just standing before them. This is not Aurobindo. This is the bioplasma. Aurobindo is gone, but the bioplasma, the *pranamay kosh*, can persist for centuries. If the person has been really in tune with his *pranamay kosh*, it can persist. It can have its own existence.

Natural breathing has to be understood. Watch small children – they breathe naturally. That's why small children are so full of energy; the parents are tired, but they are not tired.

One child was saying to another child, "I am so full of energy that I wear out my shoes within seven days."

Another said, "That's nothing. I am so full of energy I wear out my clothes within three days."

The third said, "That too is nothing. I am so full of energy I wear out my parents within one hour."

In America they have done an experiment: one very powerful man – an athletic body with tremendous energy – was told to follow a small child and imitate. Whatsoever the child does, this athlete has to do; just imitate for eight hours. Within four hours the athlete was gone, flat on the floor, because the child enjoyed it very much and he started doing many things – jumping, jogging, shouting, yelling. And the athlete has just to repeat… The child was perfectly full of energy after four hours; the athlete was gone. He said, "He will kill me. Eight hours! Finished! I cannot do anything more." He was a great boxer, but boxing is one thing. You cannot compete with a child.

From where does the energy come? It comes from *pranamay kosh*. A child breathes naturally, and of course breathes more *prana* in, more chi in and accumulates it in his belly. The belly is the accumulating place, the reservoir. Watch a child; that is the right way to breathe. When a child breathes, his chest is completely unaffected. His belly goes up and down. He breathes as if from the belly. All children have a little belly; that belly is there because of their breathing and the reservoir of energy.

That is the right way to breathe; remember not to use your chest too much. Sometimes it can be used, in emergency periods – you are running to save your life – then the chest can be used. It is an emergency device; then you can use shallow, fast breathing, and run. But ordinarily the chest should not be used. And one thing to be remembered: because the chest is meant only for emergency situations, because it is difficult in an emergency situation to breathe naturally – if you breathe naturally you remain so calm and quiet you cannot run, you cannot fight, you are so calm and collected you are buddhalike... And in an emergency – the house is on fire – if you breathe naturally, you will not be able to save anything. Or if a tiger jumps upon you in a forest and you go on breathing naturally you will not be bothered. You will say, "Okay, let him do whatsoever he wants." You will not be able to protect yourself.

So nature has given an emergency device; the chest is an emergency device. When a tiger attacks you, you have to drop natural breathing and you have to breathe by the chest. Then you will have more capacity to run, to fight, to burn energy fast. And in an emergency situation there are only two alternatives – flight or fight. Both need a very shallow but intense energy – shallow but a very disturbed, tense state.

Now if you continuously breathe from the chest, you will have tensions in your mind. If you continuously breathe from the chest, you will always be afraid because the chest breathing is meant only in fearful situations. And if you have made it a habit then you will be continuously afraid, tense, always in flight. The enemy is not there, but you will imagine the enemy is there; that's how paranoia is created.

In the West also, a few people have come across this phenomenon – Alexander Lowen and other bioenergetic people who have been working on bioenergy. That is *prana*. They have come to feel that in people who are afraid, the chest is tense and they are breathing very shallow breaths. If their breathing can be made deeper, to go and touch the belly, the hara center, then their fear disappears. If their musculature can be relaxed, as is done in Rolfing… Ida Rolf has invented one of the most beautiful methods to change the inner structure of the body because if you have been breathing wrongly for many years, you have developed a musculature, and that musculature will be in the way and will not allow you to rightly breathe or deeply breathe. And even if you remember for a few seconds and breathe deeply – again when you are engaged in your work you will start shallow-chest breathing. The musculature has to be changed. Once the musculature is changed, the fear disappears and the tension disappears. Rolfing is tremendously helpful; but also working on *pranamay kosh*, the second bioplasma body, bioenergy body, chi body, or whatsoever you want to call it.

Watch a child; *that* is natural breathing and breathe that way. Let your belly come up when you inhale, let your belly go down when you exhale. And let it be in such a rhythm it becomes almost a song in your energy, a dance – with rhythm, with harmony – and you will feel so relaxed, so alive, so vital that you cannot imagine that such vitality is possible.

Then is the third body, *manomay kosh* – the mental body. The third is bigger than the second, subtler than the second, higher than the second. Animals have the second body but not the third. Animals are so vital: see a lion walking – what beauty, what grace, what grandeur! Man has always felt jealous. See a deer running – what weightlessness, what energy, what a great energy phenomenon! Man has always felt jealous, but man's energy is moving higher.

The third body is *manomay kosh*, the mental body. This is bigger, more spacious than the second. And if you don't grow it, you will remain just a possibility of man but not a real man. The word *man* comes from *man*, *manomay*. The English word also comes from the Sanskrit root *man*. The Hindi word for man is *manushya*; that too comes from the same root *man*, the mind. It is mind that makes you man, but more or less you don't have it. What you have in its place is just a conditioned mechanism. You live by imitation: then you don't have a mind. When you start living on your own – spontaneous – when you start answering your life problems on your own, when you become responsible, you start growing in *manomay kosh*. Then the mind-body grows.

Ordinarily if you are a Hindu or a Mohammedan or a Christian you have a borrowed mind; it is not your mind. Maybe Christ attained to a great explosion of *manomay kosh* and then people have been simply repeating it. That repetition will not become a growth in you. That repetition will be a hindrance. Don't repeat: rather try to understand. Become more and more alive, authentic, responsive. Even if there is a possibility to go astray, go astray. Because there is no way to grow if you are so afraid of committing errors. Errors are good; mistakes have to be committed. Never commit the same mistake again, but never be afraid of committing mistakes. People who become so afraid of committing mistakes never grow. They go on sitting in their place, afraid to move. They are not alive.

The mind grows when you face, encounter, situations on your own. You bring your own energy to solve them. Don't go asking for advice forever. Take the reins of your life in your own hands; that's what I mean when I say do your thing. You will be in trouble – it is safer to follow others, it is convenient to follow the society, to follow the routine, the tradition, the scripture. It is very easy because everybody is following – you have just to become a dead part of the herd, you have just to move with the crowd wherever it is going; it is none of your responsibility. But your mental body, your *manomay kosh*, will suffer tremendously, terribly; it will not grow. You will not have your own mind, and you will miss something very, very beautiful and something which functions as a bridge for higher growth.

So always remember, whatsoever I say to you, you can take it in two ways. You can simply take it on my authority: "Osho says so, it must be true" – then you will suffer, then you will not grow. Whatsoever I say, listen to it, try to understand it, implement it in your life, see how it works, and then come to your own conclusions. They may be the same, they may not be. They can never be exactly the same because you have a different personality, a unique being. Whatsoever I am saying is my own. It is bound to be in deep ways rooted in me. You may come to similar conclusions, but they cannot be exactly the same. So my conclusions should not be made your conclusions. You should try to understand me, you should try to learn, but you should not collect knowledge from me, you should not collect conclusions from me. Then your mind-body will grow.

But people take shortcuts. They say, "If you have known, finished. What is the need for us to try and experiment? We will believe in you." A believer has no *manomay kosh*. He has a false *manomay kosh* which has not come out of his own being but has been forced from without.

Then higher than *manomay kosh*, bigger than *manomay kosh*, is *vigyanamay kosh* – it is the intuitive body. It is very, very spacious. Now there is no reason in it; it goes beyond reason, has become very, very subtle. It is an intuitive grasp. It is a *seeing* directly into the nature of things. It is not trying to think about it.

The cypress tree in the courtyard: you just look at it. You don't think about it; there is no "about" in intuition. You simply become available, receptive, and reality reveals to you its nature. You don't project. You are not searching for any argument, for any conclusion, nothing whatsoever. You are not even searching. You are simply waiting, and reality reveals – it is a revelation. The intuitive body takes you to very far out horizons, but still there is one body more.

That is the fifth body, *anandmay kosh* – the bliss body. That is really far out! It is made of pure bliss. Even intuition is transcended.

These five seeds are just seeds, remember. Beyond these five is *your* reality. These are just seeds surrounding you: the first is very gross; you are almost confined in a six-foot body. The second is bigger than it, the third still bigger, the fourth still bigger, the fifth is very big; but still these are seeds. All are limited. If all the seeds are dropped and you stand nude in your reality, then you are infinite. That's what yoga says: you are godly – *aham brahmasmi*. You are the very *brahman*. Now you are ultimate reality itself; now all barriers are dropped.

Try to understand this. The barriers are there surrounding you in circles. The first barrier is very, very hard. To get out of it is very difficult. People remain confined to their physical bodies and they think their physical life is all that there is to life.

Don't settle… The physical body is just a step to the energy body. The energy body is again just a step for the mind body. That too in its own, just a step for the intuitive body. That too, a step for the bliss body. And from bliss you take the jump – now there are no more steps – you take the jump into the abyss of your being that is infinity, eternity.

These are five seeds.

Corresponding to these five seeds, yoga has another doctrine about five *bhutas*, five great elements. Just as your body is made of food, earth; the earth is the first element. It has nothing to do with this earth, remember. The element simply says wherever there is matter it is earth; the material is the earth, the gross is the earth. In you it is the body; outside you it is the body of all. The stars are made of earth. Everything that exists is made of earth. The first shell is of earth. Five *bhutas* means five great elements: earth, fire, water, air, ether.

Earth corresponds to your first, *annamay kosh*, the food body. Fire corresponds to your second body, energy body, bioplasma, chi, *pranamay kosh*; it has the quality of fire. Third is water. It corresponds to the third, *manomay* body, the mental body; it has the quality of water. Watch the mind, how it goes on like a flux, always moving, moving riverlike. The fourth is air, almost invisible; you cannot see it but it is there. You can only feel it. That corresponds to the intuitive body, *vigyanamay kosh*. And then there *is akash*, ether; you cannot even feel it. It has become even more subtle than air. You can simply believe it, trust it that it is there. It is pure space; that is bliss.

But you are purer than pure space, subtler than pure space. Your reality is almost as if it is not. That's why Buddha says *anatta* – no-self. Your self is like a no-self; your being is almost like a nonbeing. Why nonbeing? Because it has gone so far away from all gross elements. It is pure is-ness. Nothing can be said about it, no description will be adequate for it.

These are five *bhutas*, five great elements, corresponding to five *koshs*, bodies, within you.

Then the third doctrine – I would like you to understand all these because they will be helpful in understanding the sutras that we will be discussing now. Then there are seven chakras. The word *chakra* does not really mean center; the word *center* cannot explain it or describe it or translate it rightly because when we say "the center," it seems something static. And *chakra* means something dynamic. The word *chakra* means "the wheel," the moving wheel. So a chakra is a dynamic center in your being, almost like a whirlpool, whirlwind, the center of the cyclone. It is dynamic; it creates an energy field around it.

Seven chakras. The first is a bridge and the last is also a bridge; the remaining five correspond to five *mahabhutas*, the great elements and the five seeds. Sex is a bridge, a bridge between you and the grossest – the *prakriti*, nature. *Sahasrar*, the seventh chakra is also a bridge, a bridge between you and the abyss – the ultimate. These two are bridges. The remaining five centers correspond to five elements and five bodies.

This is the framework of Patanjali's system. Remember it is arbitrary. It has to be used as a tool, not discussed as a dogma. It is not a doctrine in any theology. It is just a utilitarian map. You go to some territory, to some strange country, unknown, and you take a map with you. The map does not really represent the territory; how can the map represent the territory? The map is so small, the territory is so big. On the map, cities are just points. How can those points correspond to big cities? On the map, roads are just lines. How can roads be just lines? Mountains are just marked, rivers are just marked – and small ones are left out. Only big ones are marked. This is a map; it is not a doctrine.

There are not only five bodies, there are many bodies because between two bodies there is another to join it, and so on and so forth. You are like an onion, layers upon layers, but these five will do. These are the main bodies, the chief ones. So don't be too worried about it – because Buddhists say there are seven bodies, and Jainas say there are nine bodies. Nothing wrong and there is no contradiction because these are just maps. If you are studying the whole world's map, then even big cities disappear, even big rivers disappear. If you are studying a map of a nation, then many new things appear which were not on the world map. And if you are studying the map of a province, then many more things appear. And if you are studying the map of a district, of course many more. And if just of one city, then many more, and if just of one house, then of course things go on appearing, it depends.

Jainas say nine. Buddha says seven. Patanjali says five. There are schools which say only three. And they all are true because they are not discussing any argument, they are just giving you a few tools to work with.

And I think five is almost perfect because more than five is too much, less than five is too few. Five seems almost perfect, and Patanjali is a very balanced thinker.

Now a few things about these chakras: The first chakra, the first dynamic center, is sex – *muladhar*. It joins you with nature, it joins you with the past, it joins you with the future. You were born out of two persons' sexual play. Your parents' sexual play became the cause of your birth. You are related to your parents through the sex center, and to your parents' parents and so on and so forth. You are related to the whole past through the sex center. The thread runs through the sex center and if you give birth to a child, you will be related to the future.

Jesus insists many times, in a very rude way, "If you don't hate your mother and your father, you cannot come and follow me." It looks almost hard, almost unbelievable that a man like Jesus… Why should he use such hard words? And he is compassion incarnate, and he is love. Why does he say, "Hate your mother, hate your father if you want to follow me"? The meaning is: drop out of the sexual context. What he is saying symbolically is go beyond the sex center, then immediately you are no longer related with the past, no longer related with the future.

It is sex that makes you part of time. Once you go beyond sex, you become part of eternity, not of time. Then suddenly only the present exists. You are the present but if you see yourself through the sex center, you are the past also because your eyes will have the color of your mother and your father, and your body will have atoms and cells from millions of generations. Your whole structure, biostructure, is part of a long continuum. You are part of a big chain.

In India, they say your debt to your parents cannot be

fulfilled unless you give birth to children. If you want that your debt should be fulfilled with the past, you have to create the future. If you really want to repay, there is no other way. Your mother loved you, your father loved you – what can you do now they are gone? You can become a mother, a father to children and repay it to nature – to the same reservoir from where your parents came, you came, your children will come.

Sex is the great chain. It is the whole chain of the world, samsara, and it is the link with others. Have you watched it? The moment you feel sexual you start thinking of the other; when you are not feeling sexual you never think of the other. A person who is beyond sex is beyond others. He may live in the society, but he is not in the society. He may be walking in the crowd, but he walks alone. And a man who is sexual may be sitting on the top of Everest, alone, but he will think of the other. He may be sent to the moon to meditate, but he will meditate about the other.

Sex is the bridge with the others. Once sex disappears the chain is broken. For the first time you become an individual. That's why people may be too obsessed with sex, but they are never happy with it because it is double-edged. It links you with others, it does not allow you to be individual. It does not allow you to be yourself. It forces you into patterns, into slaveries, bondages. But if you don't know how to transcend it, that's the only way to use your energy – it becomes a safety valve.

People who live at the first center, *muladhar*, live only for a very foolish reason. They go on creating energy and then they are too burdened with it. Then they go on throwing it away. They eat, they work, they sleep, they do many things to create energy. Then they say, "What to do with it? It is very heavy." Then they throw it – seems a very vicious circle! When they throw it away, they again feel empty. They fill with new fuel, with new food, with new work, and again when the energy is there they are "feeling too full," they say. Somewhere it has to be released. And sex becomes just a release: a vicious circle of accumulating energy, throwing energy, accumulating energy, throwing energy. It looks almost absurd.

Unless you know that there are higher centers within you that can take that energy – use it in a creative way – you will remain confined to the sexual vicious circle. That's why all the religions insist on some sort of sexual control. It can become repressive, it can become dangerous. If new centers are not opening and you go on damming energy, condemning, forcing, repressing, then you are on a volcano. Any day you will explode; you will become neurotic. You are going to be mad. Then it is better to relieve it. But there are centers which can absorb the energy, and greater being and greater possibilities can be revealed to you.

Remember, we have been saying in the past few days that the second center, near the sex center, is the hara, the center of death. That's why people are afraid to move beyond sex because the moment the energy moves beyond sex it touches the hara center and one becomes afraid. That's why people are even afraid to move deeply in love because when you move deeply into love, the sex center creates such ripples that the ripples enter the hara center and fear arises.

So many people come to me and they say, "Why do we feel so afraid of the other sex?" – of men or women – "Why do we feel so afraid?" It is not the fear of the other sex, it is the fear of sex itself because if you go deeply into sex, then the center becomes more dynamic, creates bigger energy fields and those energy fields start overlapping with the hara center. Have you watched? In a sexual orgasm something starts moving just below your navel, throbbing. That throb is the overlapping of the sex center with the hara. That's why people become afraid of sex also. Particularly people become afraid of deep intimacy, of orgasm itself.

But that second center has to be entered, penetrated, opened. That's the meaning when Jesus says unless you are ready to die, you cannot be reborn.

Just a few days ago, on Easter, somebody has asked a question, "Today is Easter, have you something to say?" I have only one thing to say, that each day is Easter because Easter is the day of Jesus' resurrection – his crucifixion and resurrection, his death and his being reborn. Each day is an Easter if you are ready to move into the hara center. You will be crucified first – the cross is there within your hara center. You are already carrying it; you just have to move to it and you have to die through it, and then there is resurrection.

Once you die in the hara center, death disappears; then for the first time you become aware of a new world, a new dimension. Then you can see the center higher than the hara; that is the navel center. And the navel center becomes the resurrection because it is the most energy-conserving center. It is the very reservoir of energy.

And once you know that you have moved from the sex center to the hara, now you know that there is a possibility of moving inward. You have opened one door. Now you cannot rest unless you have opened all the doors. Now you cannot remain on the porch; you have entered the palace. Then you can open another door and another door…

Just in the middle is the heart center. The heart center divides the lower and the higher. First is the sex center, then the hara, then the navel, and then comes the heart center. Three centers are below it, three centers are above it: The heart is exactly in the middle.

You must have seen Solomon's seal. In Judaism, particularly in Cabalistic thinking, Solomon's seal is one of the most important symbols. That Solomon's seal is the symbol of the heart center. Sex moves downward, so sex is like a triangle pointed downward. *Sahasrar* moves upward, so *sahasrar* is a triangle moving upward, pointed upward. And the heart is just in the middle, where the sex triangle comes to meet the *sahasrar* triangle. Both triangles meet, merge into each other, and it becomes a six-pointed star, that is the seal of Solomon. The heart is the seal of Solomon.

Once you have opened the heart, then you are available for the highest possibilities. Below the heart you remain man; beyond the heart you have become superman.

After the heart center there is the throat center, then there is the third-eye center, and then *sahasrar*.

The heart is feeling love. The heart is absorbing love, becoming love. The throat is expression, communication, sharing, giving it to others. And if you give love to others, then the third-eye center starts functioning. Once you start giving, you go higher and higher. A person who goes on taking goes lower and lower and lower. A person who goes on giving goes higher and higher and higher. A miser is the worst possibility a man can fall into, and a sharer is the greatest possibility that a man can become available to.

Five bodies, five *mahabhutas*, and five centers, plus two bridges; this is the framework, the map. Behind this framework is the whole effort of the yogi, of bringing *samyama* to every nook and corner, so one becomes enlightened, full of light.

Now the sutras of Patanjali – he says:

The power of contacting the state of consciousness
which is outside the mental body, manomay sharir,
and therefore inconceivable
is called mahavideha.
Through this power
the covering of the light is destroyed.

Once you are beyond the mind-body, for the first time you become aware that you are not the mind but the witness. Below the mind you remain identified with it. Once you know that thoughts, mental images, ideas, are just objects, floating clouds in your consciousness – you are separate from them immediately.

The power of contacting the state of consciousness which is outside the mental body and therefore inconceivable is called *mahavideha.* You become beyond body. *Mahavideha* means one who is beyond body, one who is no longer confined to any body, one who knows that he is not the body, gross or subtle, one who knows that he is infinite, with no boundaries. *Mahavideha* means one who has come to feel that he has no boundaries. All boundaries are confinements, imprisonments; and he can break them, drop them, and he can become one with the infinite sky.

This moment of realizing oneself as the infinite is the moment: *through this power the covering of the light is destroyed.* Then the covering is dropped which has been hiding your light. You are like a light which is being hidden under covers and covers, by and by each and every cover has to be taken away; more light will penetrate out of it.

Manomay kosh, the mental body, once dropped you become meditation, you become a no-mind. All our effort here is how to go beyond the *manomay kosh* – how to become aware: "I am not the thinking process."

*Performing samyama on their gross, constant,
subtle, all-pervading, and functional state
brings mastery over the panchabhutas –
the five elements.*

This is one of the most potential sutras of Patanjali, and very significant for future science. One day or other, science is going to discover the meaning of this sutra.

Science is already on the path toward it. This sutra says that all the elements in the world, the *pancha mahabhutas* – earth, air, fire, etcetera – they come out of nothing, and they go again into nothingness to rest. Everything comes out of nothing and when tired, goes back and rests into nothingness.

Now science, particularly physicists, agree with it: that matter has come out of nothing. The deeper they have gone into matter, the more they have discovered that there is nothing like the material. The deeper they go, matter becomes more and more elusive and finally it slips out of their fingers. Nothing remains, just emptiness, just pure space. Out of pure space everything is born. Looks very illogical – but life is illogical. The whole of modern science has become illogical because if you persist in your logic, you cannot move into reality. If you move into reality you have to drop logic. And of course when there is a choice between logic and reality, how can you choose logic? You have to drop logic.

Just fifty years ago, scientists came to realize that quanta, electric particles, behave in a very ridiculous way, behave like a Zen master – unbelievable, absurd – sometimes they look like waves and sometimes they look like particles. Now before that it was a tacit understanding that something can be *either* a particle or a wave. One and the same thing cannot be both together, simultaneously. A particle and a wave? It means something can be a point and a line together, at the same time. Impossible! Euclid will not agree. Aristotle will simply deny – you have gone mad. A point is a point, and a line is many points in a row, so how can one point be a line also at the same time remaining a point? Looks absurd – and Euclid and Aristotle prevailed.

Just fifty years before, their whole edifice collapsed because scientists came to know that the quantum, the electric particle, behaves in both ways simultaneously.

Logicians raised arguments, and they said, "This is not possible." Physicists said, "What can we do? It is not a question of possibility or impossibility. It is so! We cannot do anything. If the quantum is not going to follow Aristotle, what can we do? And if the quantum behaves in a non-Euclidean way and does not follow the geometry of Euclid, what can we do? We have to listen to the behavior of the real and the reality."

This is one of the very critical moments in the history of human consciousness. It has always been believed that something can come only out of something. Simple and natural, obviously so. How can something come out of nothing? Then matter disappeared, and the scientists have to conclude that everything is born out of nothing, and everything disappears again into nothing. Now they are talking about black holes. Black holes are holes of tremendous nothingness. I have to call it "tremendous nothingness" because that nothingness is not just an absence. It is full of energy, but the energy is of nothingness. There is nothing to find, but there is energy.

Now they say there exist black holes in existence. They are parallel to stars – stars are positive, and parallel to each star there is a black hole. The star is; the black hole is not. Each star when burned, exhausted, becomes a black hole. And each black hole, when rested, becomes a star.

Matter, no-matter go on changing. Matter becomes no-matter; no-matter becomes matter. Life becomes death; death becomes life. Love becomes hate; hate becomes love. Polarities continuously change.

This sutra says, *Performing* samyama *on their gross, constant, subtle, all-pervading, and functional state brings mastery over the* panchabhutas – *the five elements*. Patanjali is saying that if you have come to understand your true nature of witnessing, and then if you concentrate – you bring *samyama* on any matter – you can make it appear or disappear. You can help things to materialize because they come out of nothingness. And you can help things to dematerialize.

Now, that yet remains to be seen by physicists, whether it is possible or not. It is happening that matter changes and becomes no-matter, no-matter changes, becomes matter. They have come to feel many absurd things these fifty years. It is one of the most potential ages ever, where so many things have exploded that it has become almost impossible to confine them in a system. How to make a system? It was very easy just fifty years earlier to create a self-contained system and now it is impossible. Reality has poked its nose from everywhere and destroyed all doctrinaires, systems, dogmas. Reality has proved to be too much.

Scientists say it is happening. Patanjali says it can be made to happen. If it is happening, then why can it not be made to happen? Just watch. You heat water; at a hundred degrees it becomes vapor. It has always been happening, before fire was ever discovered. The sun rays were evaporating water from the seas and rivers, and clouds were forming and water was coming back again into the rivers, again evaporating. Then man discovered fire, and then he started heating water, evaporating it.

Whatever is happening, ways and means can be found to make it happen. If it is already happening then it is not against reality, then you have just to know how to make it happen. If matter becomes no-matter, no-matter becomes matter, if things change polarities, things disappear into nothingness and things appear out of nothingness – if this is already happening – then Patanjali says ways and means can be found through which it can be made to happen. And this he says is the way: if you have come to recognize your being, beyond the five seeds, you become capable of materializing things or dematerializing things.

It still remains for the scientific workers to find out whether it is possible or not, but it seems plausible. There seems to be no logical problem in it.

> *From this follows the attainment of anima, etcetera,*
> *Perfection of the body, and*
> *the removal of the elements' power to obstruct the body.*

And then come the eight *siddhis*, eight powers of yogis. The first is *anima*, and then there is *laghima* and *garima*, etcetera. The eight powers of the yogi are that they can make their body disappear, or they can make their body so small, so small that it becomes almost invisible, or they can make their bodies so big, as big as they want. It is under their control to make the body small, big, or disappear completely, or to appear in many places simultaneously.

Looks impossible, but things that look impossible by and by become possible. It was impossible for man to fly; nobody ever believed – the Wright brothers were thought to be mad, insane. When they invented their first airplane, they were so afraid to tell people – that if people come to know, they would be caught and hospitalized. The first flight was done completely unknown to anybody, just these two brothers. And they invented their first airplane hiding in a basement, so nobody came to know what they were doing. Everybody had believed that they had gone completely mad – who has ever flown? Their first air flight was of sixty seconds only – only of sixty seconds – but it changed the whole of history tremendously, the whole of humanity. It became possible.

Nobody had ever thought that the atom could be split. It was split, and now man can never be the same again.

Many things have happened which were always thought to be impossible. We have reached the moon; it was the symbol of impossibility. In all the languages of the world there are expressions like, "Don't long for the moon." That means don't long for the impossible. Now we have to change those expressions. And in fact, once we have reached the moon, now nothing debars the path. Now everything has become available; it is only a question of time.

Einstein has said that if we can invent a vehicle which moves with the speed of light, then a person can go on traveling and he will never age. If he goes on a spaceship that moves with the speed of light when he is thirty years old, and comes back after thirty years, he will remain thirty years old. His friends and brothers will be sixty years old, a few of them will be already dead, but the person will remain thirty years old. What nonsense are you saying? Einstein says time and its effect disappear when one is moving with the speed of light. A man can go on infinite space travel and can come back after five hundred years. All the people here will be gone, nobody will recognize him and he will not recognize anybody, but he will remain the same age. You are aging because of the speed of the earth. If the speed is as much as light, which is really tremendous, then you will not age at all.

Patanjali says that if you have moved beyond all the five bodies, you have gone beyond all five elements. Now you are in a state from where you can control anything you wish. Just by the idea that you want to become small, you will become small; if you want to become big, you will become big; if you want to disappear, you can disappear.

It is not necessarily that yogis should do it. Buddhas have never been known to do it. Patanjali himself has not been known to do it. What Patanjali is saying – he is revealing all the possibilities.

In fact, a man who has attained his uttermost being, for what will he think to become small? For what? He can't be so foolish. For what? For what would he like to become like an elephant? What is the point in it? And why should he want to disappear? He cannot be interested in amusing people, their curiosities. He is not a magician. He is not interested in people applauding him. For what? In fact, the moment a person reaches the highest peak of his being, all desires disappear. *Siddhis* appear when desires disappear. This is the dilemma: powers come when you don't want to use them. In fact, they come only when the person has disappeared who always wanted to have them.

This part of Patanjali's *Yoga Sutras* is to make you aware that these things become possible but they are never actualized because the person who would want it, who would have always liked to go on an ego trip through these powers, is no longer there. Miraculous powers happen to you when you are not interested in them. This is the economy of existence. If you desire, you remain impotent. If you don't desire, you become infinitely potent. This I call the law of banking: if you don't have money, no bank is going to give you any; if you have money, every bank is ready to give you more. When you don't need, all is available; when you are needy, nothing is available.

*Beauty, grace, strength, and adamantine hardness
constitute the perfect body.*

Patanjali is not talking about *this* body. This body can be beautiful, but can never be perfectly beautiful. The second body can be more beautiful than this, the third even more, because they are moving closer to the center. The beauty is of the center. The farther away it has to travel, the more limited it becomes. The fourth body is even more beautiful. The fifth is almost ninety-nine percent perfect.

But that which is your being – the real you – is beauty, grace, strength, and adamantine hardness. It is adamantine hardness and at the same time the softness of a lotus. It is beautiful but not fragile – strong. It is strong, but not just hard – all opposites meet in it, as if a lotus flower is made of diamonds or a diamond is made of lotus flowers; because man and woman meet there and transcend, because sun and moon meet there and transcend.

The old term for yoga is *hatha*. This word *hatha* is very, very significant. *Ha* means sun, *tha* means moon; and *hatha* means the meeting of the sun and the moon. The union of sun and moon is yoga – *unio mystica*.

In the human body, according to the *hatha* yogis, there are three channels of energy. One is known as *pingala*; that is the right channel, connected with the left brain – the sun channel. Then there is another channel *ida*; the left channel, connected with the right brain – the moon channel. And then there is the third channel, the middle channel, *sushumna*; the central, the balanced – it is made of the sun and the moon together.

Ordinarily your energy moves either by the *pingala* or by *ida*. Yogis' energy starts moving through the *sushumna*. That is called kundalini, when the energy moves just between these two, right and left. These channels exist corresponding to your backbone. Once the energy moves in the middle channel, you become balanced. Then a person is neither a man nor a woman, neither hard nor soft; or both – man and woman, hard and soft. All the polarities disappear in *sushumna*; and *sahasrar* is the peak of *sushumna*.

If you live on the lowest point of your being, that is *muladhar*, the sex center, then either you move by *ida* or you move by *pingala*, the sun channel or the moon channel; and you remain divided. And you go on seeking the other, you go on asking for the other – you feel incomplete in yourself, you have to depend on the other.

Once your own energies meet inside, a great orgasm happens, a cosmic orgasm – when the *ida* and *pingala* dissolve into *sushumna* – then one is thrilled, eternally thrilled. Then one is ecstatic, continuously ecstatic; then that ecstasy knows no end. Then one never comes down, then one never comes low; one remains high. That point of highness becomes one's innermost core, one's very being.

Remember again, I would like to say to you: this is the framework. We are not talking about actual things. There are foolish people who have even tried to dissect the human body to see where *ida* is and *pingala* is, and, "Where is *sushumna*?" They have found them nowhere. These are just indicators, symbolic.

There are foolish people who have tried to dissect the body and to find where the centers are. One doctor has even written a book to prove which center is exactly which complex in the body according to physiologists. These are all foolish attempts.

Yoga is not in *that* way scientific. It is allegorical. It is a great allegory. It is showing something and if you go inside you will find it, but there is no way to find it by dissecting a body. By postmortem you will not find these things. These are alive phenomena. And these words are simply indicative – don't be confined to them, and don't make a fixed obsession and doctrine out of them. Remain fluid. Take the hint, and go on the journey.

One more word; it is *urdhvaretas*. It means the upward journey of energy. Right now you are existing at the sex center, and from that center the energy goes on falling downward. *Urdhvaretas* means your energy starts moving upward. A delicate, very delicate phenomenon, and one has to be very alert to work with it. If you are not alert there is every possibility you will become a perverted being. It is dangerous; that's why yogis call it "serpent power." It is dangerous. It is like a snake – you are playing with a snake. If you don't know how to, what to do, there is danger – you are playing with poison.

And many people have become perverted because they tried to repress their sex energy in order to become *urdhvaretas*, to go upward. They never went upward. They even became more perverted than normal people.

That's why a master is needed – one who knows where you are, where you are going, and what is going to happen next; one who can see your future and one who can see whether the right channeling is happening or not. Otherwise the whole world is in a mess of sexual perversion.

Never repress. It is better to be normal and natural than to be perverted. But just to be normal is not enough, much more is possible: Transform. Repression is not the way of *urdhvaretas* – transformation is. And that can be done only if you purify your body, you purify your mind; you throw away all rubbish that you have gathered in the body and the mind. Only with a purity, light, weightlessness, will you be able to help the energy to move upward.

Ordinarily it is like a coiled snake; that's why we call it kundalini, or *kundali*. *Kundali* means "coiled up." When it raises its head and moves upward, tremendous is the experience. Whenever it passes a higher center, you will have higher and higher experiences. At each center many things will be revealed to you; you are a great book. But the energy has to pass through the centers; only then can those centers reveal to you their beauties, their visions, their poetries, their songs, their dances. And each center has a higher orgasm than the lower one.

Sexual orgasm is the lowest. Higher is the orgasm of the hara. Then higher than that is the orgasm of the *nabhi*, the navel. Then higher than that is that of love – the heart. Then higher than that is that of the throat – creativity, sharing. Then higher than that is that of the third eye, the vision of life as really it is, without any projections – the clarity to see unclouded. And highest is that of the *sahasrar*, the seventh center.

This is the map. If you want, you can move upward, become *urdhvaretas*. But never try to become *urdhvaretas* for *siddhis*, powers – they are all foolish. Try to become *urdhvaretas* to know who you are, not for power but peace. Let peace be thy goal, never power.

Patanjali called this chapter *Vibhuti Pada*; *vibhuti* means "power." included this chapter so that his disciples and those who will be following him are made alert that many powers happen on the way but you are not to get entangled with them. Once you become entangled with power, once you are on a power trip, you are in trouble. You will be tied down to that spot – and your flight will be stopped. And one has to go on flying and flying till the very end, when the abyss opens and you are absorbed back into the cosmic soul.

Let peace be thy goal.

CHAPTER 10

Tantra and the World of the Chakras

Tantra is freedom – freedom from all mind constructs, from all mind games; freedom from all structures, freedom from the other. Tantra is a space to be. Tantra is liberation.

Tantra is not a religion in the ordinary sense. Religion is again a mind game, religion gives you a certain pattern. A Christian has a certain pattern, so has a Hindu, so has a Muslim. Religion gives you a certain style, a discipline. Tantra takes all disciplines away.

When there is no discipline, when there is no enforced order, a totally different kind of order arises in you. What Lao Tzu calls Tao, what Buddha calls *dhamma*, arises in you. This is not anything done by you; it happens to you. Tantra simply creates a space for it to happen. It does not even invite, it does not wait; it simply creates a space. And when the space is ready, the whole flows in.

I have heard a very beautiful story, a very ancient one...

In a province, no rain had fallen for a long time – everything was dried up. At last the citizens decided to fetch the rainmaker. A deputation was sent to see him in the distant town where he lived, with an urgent request to come as soon as possible and make rain for their parched fields.

The rainmaker, a wise old man, promised to do so, on condition that he was provided with a solitary little cottage in the open country where he could withdraw by himself for three days – no food or drink would be required. Then he would see what could be done. His requests were met.

On the evening of the third day abundant rain fell, and full of praise, a grateful crowd made a pilgrimage to his house and exclaimed, "How did you do it? Tell us."

"It was quite simple," the rainmaker answered. "For three days all I did was to put myself in order. For, I know that once I am in order, then the world will be in order, and the drought must yield place to the rain."

Tantra says that if you are in order, then the whole world is in order for you. When you are in harmony, then the whole existence is in harmony for you. When you are in disorder, then the whole world is disorder. And the order must not be a false one, it must not be a forced one. When you force some order upon yourself, you simply become split; deep down the disorder continues.

You can observe it: if you are an angry person you can force your anger, you can repress it deep down in the unconscious, but it is not going to disappear. Maybe you become completely unaware of it, but it is there – and you know that it is there. It is running underneath you, it is in the dark basement of your being, but it is there. You can sit smiling on top of it, but you know it can erupt any moment. And your smile cannot be very deep, and your smile cannot be true, and your smile will be just an effort you are making against yourself. A man who forces order from the outside remains in disorder.

Tantra says there is another kind of order. You don't impose any order, you don't impose any discipline; you simply drop all structures, you simply become natural and spontaneous. It is the greatest step a man can be asked to take. It will need great courage because the society will not like it, the society will be dead against it. The society wants a certain order. If you follow the society, the society is happy with you. If you go a little bit astray here and there, the society is very angry – and the mob is mad.

Tantra is a rebellion. I don't call it revolutionary because it has no politics in it. And I don't call it revolutionary because it has no plans to change the world, it has no plans to change the state and the society. It is rebellious, it is individual rebellion. It is one individual slipping out of the structures and the slavery. But the moment you slip out of the slavery, you come to feel another kind of existence around you that you have never felt before – as if you were living with a blindfold and suddenly the blindfold has become loose, your eyes have opened and you can see a totally different world.

This blindfold is what you call your mind – your thinking, your prejudices, your knowledge, your scriptures; they all make up the thick layer of the blindfold. They are keeping you blind, they are keeping you dull, they are keeping you unalive.

Tantra wants you to be alive – as alive as the trees, as alive as the rivers, as alive as the sun and the moon. That is your birthright. You don't lose anything by losing the blindfold; you gain all. And if everything is to be lost in gaining it, nothing is lost. Even a single moment of utter freedom is enough to satisfy. And a long life of a hundred years, yoked like a slave, is meaningless.

To be in the world of Tantra needs courage: it is adventurous. Up to now, only a few people have been able to move on that path. But the future is very hopeful. Tantra will become more and more important. Man understands more and more what slavery is, and man also understands that no political revolution has proved revolutionary. All political revolutions finally turn into anti-revolutions. Once revolutionaries are in power they become anti-revolutionary. Power *is* anti-revolutionary. So there is a built-in mechanism in power: give anybody power and he becomes anti-revolutionary. Power creates its own world. So up to now there have been many revolutions in the world and all have failed, utterly failed; no revolution has helped. Now man is becoming aware of it.

Tantra gives a different perspective. It is not revolutionary; it is rebellious. Rebellion means individual. You can rebel alone, you need not organize a party for it. You can rebel alone, on your own. It is not a fight against society, remember; it is just going beyond society. It is not anti-social, it is asocial; it has nothing to do with society. It is not against slavery, it is for freedom – freedom to be.

Just look at your life. Are you a free man? You are not: there are a thousand and one bondages around you. You may not look at them, it is very embarrassing; you may not recognize them, it hurts. But it doesn't change the situation: you are a slave. To move into the dimension of Tantra you will have to recognize your slavery. It is very deep-rooted; it has to be dropped, and being aware of it helps you to drop it.

Don't go on pacifying yourself, don't go on consoling yourself, don't go on saying, "Everything is okay." It is not. Nothing is okay, your whole life is just a nightmare. Have a look at it! There is no poetry and no song and no dance and no love and no prayer. There is no celebration. Joy? – it is just a word in the dictionary. Bliss? – yes, you have heard about it, but you have not known anything about it. God? – in the temples, in the churches. Yes, people talk about it. Those who talk, they don't know; those who hear, they don't know. All that is beautiful seems to be meaning-less, and all that is meaningless seems to be very, very important.

A man goes on accumulating money and thinks that he is doing something very significant. Human stupidity is infinite. Beware of it, it will destroy your whole life; it has destroyed millions of people's lives down the ages. Take hold of your awareness – that is the only possibility to get out of stupidity.

Before we enter today's sutras from Saraha, the founder of Tantra, something has to be understood about Tantra's map of inner consciousness.

First: Tantra says that no man is just man, and no woman is just woman. Each man is both man and woman, and so is each woman – woman and man. Adam has Eve in him, and Eve has Adam in her. In fact, nobody is just Adam and nobody is just Eve, we are Adam-Eves. This is one of the greatest insights ever attained.

It is one of the greatest discoveries of the world because with this understanding you can move in your inner direction; otherwise you cannot move in your inner direction. Why does a man fall in love with a woman? – because he carries a woman inside him, otherwise he would not fall in love. And why do you fall in love with a certain woman? There are thousands of women, but why, suddenly, does a certain woman become most important to you, as if all other women have disappeared and that is the only woman in the world? Why? Why does a certain man attract you? Why at first sight does something suddenly click? Tantra says you are carrying an image of a woman inside you, an image of a man inside you. Each man is carrying a woman and each woman is carrying a man. When somebody on the outside fits with your inner image, you fall in love – that is the meaning of love.

You don't understand it; you simply shrug your shoulders and say, "It has happened." But there is a subtle mechanism in it. Why did it happen with a certain woman, why not with others? Your inner image fits somehow, the outer woman is similar in a way. Something just hits your inner image. You feel, "This is my woman," or "This is my man"; this feeling is what love is. But the outer woman is not going to satisfy, because no outer woman is going to completely fit with your inner woman. The reality is not that way at all. Maybe she fits a little bit – there is an appeal, a magnetism, but it will be worn out sooner or later. Soon you will recognize that there are a thousand and one things that you don't like in the woman. It will take a little time to come to know about those things.

First you will be infatuated. First the similarity will be too much, it will overwhelm you. But by and by you will see that there are a thousand and one things, details of life, that don't fit – that you are aliens, strangers. Yes, you still love her, but the love has no more infatuation, that romantic vision is disappearing. And she will also recognize that something appeals in you, but your totality is not appealing. That's why each husband tries to change the wife and each wife tries to change the husband. What are they trying to do? Why? Why does a wife continuously try to change the husband? For what? She has fallen in love with this man, then immediately she starts changing him? Now she has become aware of the dissimilarities. She wants to drop those dissimilarities; she wants to take a few chunks off this man so that he completely fits with her idea of a man. And the husband also tries – not so hard, not so stubbornly as women try because the husband becomes tired very soon – the woman hopes longer.

The woman thinks, "Today or tomorrow or the day after tomorrow – someday he will change." It takes almost twenty, twenty-five years to recognize the fact that you cannot change the other. By the age of fifty, when the woman has passed her menopause and the man too, when they are getting really old, then they become alert by and by that nothing has changed. They have tried hard, they have tried every way; the woman remains the same and the man remains the same. Nobody can change anybody. This is a great experience to come to, a great understanding.

That's why old people become more tolerant: they know that nothing can be done. That's why old people become more graceful: they know that things are as they are. That's why old people become more accepting. Young people are very angry, nonaccepting; they want to change everything: they want to make the world the way they would like it. They struggle hard, but it has never happened. It cannot happen, it is not in the nature of things.

The outer man can never fit with your inner man, and the outer woman can never be absolutely the same as your inner woman. That's why love gives pleasure and also pain, love gives happiness and also unhappiness. And the unhappiness is much more than the happiness. What does Tantra propose about it, what has to be done then?

Tantra says that there is no way to be satisfied with the outer; you will have to move inward. You will have to find your inner woman and inner man; you will have to attain to a sexual intercourse inside. That is a great contribution.

How can it happen? Try to understand this map. I have talked about seven chakras, the Yoga-Tantra physiology. In man the *muladhar* is male and *svadhishthan*, female. In woman the *muladhar* is female and the *svadhishthan*, male, and so on and so forth. In seven chakras, up to the sixth, the duality remains; the seventh is nondual.

There are three pairs inside you: the *muladhar-svadhishthan* have to marry; the *manipura-anahata* have to marry; the *vishuddha-agya* have to marry.

When the energy moves outside, you need a woman outside. You have a little glimpse for a moment – because the coition with a woman outside cannot be permanent, it can be only momentary. For a single moment you can lose yourself in each other. Again you are thrown back to yourself, and thrown back with a vengeance. That's why after each lovemaking, there is a certain frustration: you have failed again, it didn't happen the way you wanted it to happen. Yes, you reached to a peak, but before you had even become aware of it, the decline, the fall began. Before the peak was achieved, the valley. Before you had met the woman or the man, the separation. Divorce comes so fast with marriage that it is frustrating. All lovers are frustrated people: they hope much, they hope against their experience, they hope again and again – but nothing can be done. You cannot destroy the laws of reality. You have to understand those laws.

The outer meeting can only be momentary, but the inner meeting can become eternal. And the higher you move, the more eternal it can become. The first chakra, the *muladhar*, in man is male. Even while making love to a woman outside, Tantra says, remember the inner. Make love to the woman outside, but remember the inner. Let your consciousness move inward. Forget the outer woman completely. In the moment of orgasm forget the woman or the man completely. Close your eyes and be in, and let it be a meditation. When energy is stirred, don't miss this opportunity. That is the moment when you can have a contact – an inward journey.

Ordinarily it is difficult to look in; but in a love moment there is some gap, you are not ordinary. In a love moment you are at your maximum. When orgasm happens, your whole body energy is throbbing with dance; each cell, each fiber dancing in a rhythm, in a harmony, that you don't know in ordinary life. This is the moment, this moment of harmony; use it as a passage inward. While making love, become meditative, look in.

A door opens at that moment – this is the Tantra experience. A door opens in that moment, and Tantra says that you feel happy only because that door opens and something of your inner bliss flows to you. It is not coming from the outer woman, it is not coming from the outer man; it is coming from your innermost core. The outer is just an excuse.

Tantra does not say that to make love to the outer is sin, it simply says that it is not very far-reaching. It does not condemn it, it accepts its naturalness, but it says that you can use that love wave to go far inside. In that moment of thrill, things are not on the earth: you can fly. Your arrow can lead the bow toward the target.

If while making love you become meditative, you become

silent, you start looking in, you close your eyes, you forget the outer man or woman, then it happens. The *muladhar*, your male center inside, starts moving toward the female center – the female center is the *svadhishthan* – and there is a coition, there is an intercourse inside.

Sometimes it happens without your knowing it. One man writes to me again and again, and he must be wondering why I do not answer. The map was not available up to now, now I am giving you the map. Listening to me he always feels as if he is going into orgasm. His whole body starts throbbing, and he has the same experience as he has while making love to a woman. He becomes very puzzled – naturally so. He loses track of what he was listening to – he forgets, and the thrill is so much and the joy is so much that he is worried. What is happening? What is this inside him?

This is happening: the *muladhar* is meeting with the *svadhishthan*, your male center is meeting with your female center. This is the joy when you move into meditation, when you move into prayer; this is the mechanism of your inner celebration. And the moment the *muladhar* and *svadhishthan* meet, the energy is released. Just as when you love your woman, energy is released, when the *svadhishthan* and *muladhar* meet, energy is released and that energy hits the higher center, the *manipura.*

The *manipura* is male, the *anahata* is female. Once you have become attuned to the first meeting of your man and woman inside, one day the second meeting suddenly happens. You do not have to do anything about it; just the energy released from the first meeting creates the possibility for the second meeting. And when energy is created by the second meeting, it creates the possibility for the third meeting.

The third meeting is between the *vishuddha* and *agya.* And when the third meeting happens, the energy is created for the fourth, which is not a meeting, which is not a union, but unity. The *sahasrar* is alone; there is no male-female. Adam and Eve have disappeared into each other totally, utterly. Man has become the woman, the woman has become the man; all division disappears. This is the absolute, the eternal meeting. This is what Hindus call *sat-chit-anand*. This is what Jesus calls "the Kingdom of God."

In fact the number seven has been used by all the religions. Seven days are symbolic and the seventh day is the holiday, the holy day. Six days God worked and on the seventh day he rested. You will have to work on six chakras, the seventh is the state of great rest, utter rest, absolute relaxation – you have come home.

With the seventh you disappear as part of duality; all polarities disappear, all distinctions disappear. Night is no longer night, and day is no longer day. Summer is no longer summer, and winter is no longer winter. Matter is no longer matter, and mind is no longer mind – you have gone beyond. This is the transcendental space Buddha calls nirvana.

These three meetings inside you, and the achievement of the fourth, have another dimension too. I have talked to you many times about four states: sleep, dream, waking, *turiya*. *Turiya* means "the fourth," "the beyond." These seven chakras, and the work through them, have a correspondence with these four states also.

The first meeting between the *muladhar* and *svadhishthan* is like sleep. The meeting happens, but you cannot be very aware of it. You will enjoy it, you will feel a great freshness arising in you. You will feel great rest, as if you have slept deeply; but you will not be able to see it exactly – it is very dark. The man and woman have met inside you, but they have met in the unconscious; the meeting was not in the daylight, it was in the dark night. Yes, the result will be felt, the consequence will be felt. You will suddenly feel a new energy in you, a new radiance, a new glow. You will have an aura. Even others may start feeling that you have a certain quality of presence, a vibe. But you will not be exactly alert to what is happening, so the first meeting is like sleep.

The second meeting is like dreaming: when the *manipura* and *anahata* meet, your meeting with the inner woman is as if you have met in a dream. Yes, you can remember a little bit of it, just as in the morning you can remember the dream that you had last night – a little bit here and there, a few glimpses. Maybe something has been forgotten, maybe the whole is not remembered, but still you can remember. The second meeting is like dreaming. You will become more aware of it, you will start feeling that something is happening. You will start feeling that you are changing, that a transformation is on the way, that you are no longer the old person. And with the second, you will start becoming aware that your interest in the outer woman is lessening or your interest in the outer man is not as infatuating as it used to be.

With the first there will also be a change, but you will not be aware of it. With the first you may start thinking that you are no longer interested in *your* woman, but you will not be able to understand that you are not interested in *any* woman at all. You may think you are bored with your woman and you will be happier with some other woman; a change will be good, a different climate will be good, a different quality of woman will be good. This will be just a guess. With the second you will start feeling that you are no longer interested in the woman or the man, that your interest is turning inward.

With the third you will become perfectly aware; it is like waking. The *vishuddha* meeting the *agya*: you will become perfectly aware, the meeting is happening in the daylight. Or you can say it in this way: the first meeting happens in the dark middle of the night, the second meeting happens in a twilight time between the night and the day, the third meeting happens in full noon – you are fully alert, everything is clear. Now you know you are finished with the outer. It does not mean you will leave your wife or your husband, it simply means that the infatuation is no more. You will feel compassion. Certainly the woman who has helped you so far is a great friend, the man who has brought you so far is a great friend; you are grateful. You will start being grateful and compassionate to each other.

It is always so: when understanding arises it brings compassion. If you leave your wife and escape to the forest, that simply shows you are cruel and compassion has not arisen. It can be only out of nonunderstanding, it cannot be out of understanding. If you understand you will have compassion.

When Buddha became enlightened, the first thing he said to his disciples was, "I would like to go to Yashodhara and talk to her" – his wife.

Ananda was very disturbed. He said, "What is the point of your going back to the palace and talking to your wife? You have left her – twelve years have passed." And Ananda was also a little bit disturbed because how can a buddha think about his wife? Buddhas are not expected to think that way.

When the others had left, Ananda said to Buddha, "This is not good. What will people think?"

Buddha said, "What will people think? I have to express my gratitude to her, and I have to thank her for all the help she gave me. And I have to give something of that which has happened to me – I owe that much to her. I will have to go."

He went back, he went to the palace, he saw his wife. Certainly Yashodhara was mad; this man had escaped one night without even saying anything to her. She said to Buddha, "Couldn't you have trusted me? You could have said that you wanted to go, and I would have been the last woman in the world to prevent you. Couldn't you have trusted me even that much?" And she was crying – twelve years of anger! This man had escaped like a thief in the middle of the night – suddenly, without giving a single hint to her.

Buddha apologized. And he said, "It was out of nonunder-standing. I was ignorant, I was not aware. But now I am aware and I know; that's why I have come back. You have helped me tremen-dously. Forget those old things; now there is no point in thinking about spilt milk. Look at me – something great has happened. I have come home. And I felt my first duty was toward you, to come and to convey and to share my experience with you."

The anger gone, the rage subsided, Yashodhara looked out through her tears. Yes, this man had changed tremendously; this was not the same man she used to know. This was not the same man, not at all. He looked like a great luminosity: she could almost see the aura, a light around him. And he was so peaceful and so silent; he had almost disappeared, his presence was almost absence. And then, in spite of herself, she forgot what she was doing. She fell at his feet and she asked to be initiated.

When you understand, there is bound to be compassion. That's why I don't say to my sannyasins to leave their families. Be there.

Rabindranath has written a poem about this incident – when Buddha goes. Yashodhara asked him one thing: "Just tell me one thing," she said. "Whatever you have attained – I can see you have attained, whatsoever it is, I don't know what it is – just tell me one thing: Was it not possible to attain it here in this house?"

And Buddha could not say no. It *was* possible to attain it there in the house. Now he knew, because it has nothing to do with forest or with town, with the family or with an ashram. It has nothing to do with any place; it has something to do with your innermost core. It is available everywhere.

First, you will start feeling that your interest in the other is loosening. It will be a dim phenomenon, dark – looking through a dark glass, looking through a very foggy morning. Second, things become a little clearer, like a dream, the fog is not so much. Third, you are fully awake – it has happened, the inner woman has met the inner man. The bipolarity is no longer there: suddenly you are one. Schizophrenia has disappeared, you are not split.

With this integration you become an individual. Before that you were not an individual, you were a crowd, you were a mob, you were many people, you were multi-psychic. Suddenly you fall into order. That's what this ancient story says.

The man had asked for three days... If sometimes you look into these small stories you will be wonderstruck; their symbols are great. The man had asked for three days to sit silently. Why three days? Those are the three points: in sleep, in dream, in waking; he wanted to put himself in order. First it happens in sleep, then it happens in dreams, then it happens in waking. And when you are in order, the whole of existence is in order. When you are an individual, when your split has disappeared and you are bridged together, then everything is bridged together.

It will look very paradoxical, but it has to be said: the individual is the universal. When you have become an individual, suddenly you see that you are the universal. Up to now you have been thinking that you were separate from existence; now you cannot think that. Adam and Eve have disappeared into each other. This is the goal that everybody is trying to find in some way or other. Tantra is the surest science for achieving it; this is the target.

A few more things: I told you that the *muladhar* has to be relaxed, only then can the energy move upward, inward. And inward and upward mean the same; outward and downward mean the same. Energy can move inward or upward only when the *muladhar* is relaxed. So the first thing is to relax the *muladhar*.

You are holding your sex center very tight. The society has made you very aware of the sex center; it has made you obsessed with it, so you are holding it tight. You can simply watch. You are always holding your genital organism very tight, as if you are afraid that something will go amiss if you relax. Your whole conditioning has been to keep it uptight. Relax it; leave it to itself. Don't be afraid – fear creates tension. Drop the fear. Sex is beautiful; it is not a sin, it is a virtue. Once you think in terms of its being a virtue you will be able to relax.

I have talked about how to relax the *muladhar* before. And I have talked about how to relax the *svadhishthan*; it is the death center. Don't be afraid of death. These are the two fears which have been dominating humanity: the fear of sex and the fear of death. Both fears are dangerous; they have not allowed you to grow. Drop both the fears.

The third chakra is the *manipura*; it is loaded with negative emotions. That's why your stomach becomes disturbed when you are emotionally disturbed; the *manipura* is affected immediately. In all the languages of the world we have expressions like, "I cannot stomach it." It is literally true. Sometimes when you cannot stomach a certain thing you start feeling nauseous, you would like to vomit. In fact sometimes it happens – a psychological vomit. Somebody has said something and you cannot stomach it, and suddenly you feel nausea: you vomit, and after vomiting you feel very relaxed.

In yoga they have methods for it. The yogi has to drink a large amount of water in the morning – a bucketful of water with salt; the water has to be lukewarm – and then he has to vomit it. It helps to relax the *manipura*. It is a great process, a great cleansing process.

You will be surprised: now many modern therapies have become aware of that vomiting helps. It releases the *manipura*. Tantra and yoga have always been aware of it.

The negative emotions – anger, hatred, jealousy and so forth – have all been repressed. Your *manipura* is overloaded. Those repressed emotions don't allow the energy to go up; those repressed emotions function like a rock: your passage is blocked. Encounter, Gestalt, and therapies like that, all function unknowingly on the *manipura*. They try to provoke your anger, they try to provoke your jealousy, your greed; they provoke your aggression, your violence, so that it bubbles up, surfaces. The society has done one thing: it has trained you to repress all that is negative and pretend all that is positive. Now, both are dangerous. To pretend the positive is false, hypocrisy, and to repress the negative is dangerous; it is poisonous, it is poisoning your system.

Tantra says to express the negative and allow the positive. If anger comes, don't repress it; if aggression comes, don't repress it. Tantra does not say go and kill a person – but Tantra says that there a thousand and one ways to express the repressed emotions. You can go into the garden and chop wood. Have you watched woodcutters? They look more silent than anybody else. Have you watched hunters? Hunters are very good people. They do a very dirty thing, but they are good people. Something happens to them while they are hunting. Killing animals, their anger, their aggression is dissolved. The so-called nonviolent people are the ugliest in the world. They are not good people because they are holding down a volcano. You cannot feel at ease with them; something is dangerously present there – you can feel it, you can touch it, it is oozing out of them.

You can just go into the forest and shout, scream. Primal Therapy is just scream therapy, tantrum therapy. And Encounter and Primal, Gestalt, are of tremendous help in relaxing the *manipura*.

Once the *manipura* is relaxed there arises a balance between the negative and the positive. And when the negative and positive are balanced, the passage is open; then the energy can move higher. The *manipura* is male. If the *manipura* is blocked, then energy cannot go upward. It has to be relaxed.

Anything that can be of help has to be used, because man has been so damaged that all sources of help should be made available. You may not even be able to understand why I am making available all the methods to you: Yoga, Tantra, Tao, Sufi, Jaina, Buddhist, Hindu, Gestalt, Psychodrama, Encounter, Primal

Therapy, Polarity Balancing, Rolfing, Structural Integration – why I am making all these things available to you. You have never heard of these things being done in any ashram anywhere in the East at all. There is a reason for it: man has been damaged so much that all sources should be tapped. Help should be taken from every source possible; only then there is hope. Otherwise man is doomed.

The fourth chakra is the *anahata*. Doubt is the problem with the fourth chakra; if you are a doubting person, your fourth chakra will remain unopened. Trust opens it. So anything that creates doubt destroys your heart. The *anahata* is the heart chakra. Logic, logic chopping, argumentativeness, too much rationality, too much of Aristotle in you, destroy the *anahata*. Philosophy, skepticism, destroy the *anahata*.

If you want to open the *anahata*, you will have to be more trusting. Poetry is more helpful than philosophy, and intuition is more helpful than reasoning, and feeling is more helpful than thinking. So you will have to shift from doubt to trust, only then does your *anahata* open, does your *anahata* become capable of receiving the male energy from the *manipura*. The *anahata* is female; it closes with doubt, it becomes frigid with doubt, it becomes dry with doubt – it cannot receive the male energy. It opens with trust: with trust, moisture is released in that chakra and it can allow the penetration of the male energy.

Then the fifth: the *vishuddha*. Noncreativity, imitativeness, parroting, monkeying – these are damaging.

The *vishuddha* is destroyed by copying. Don't be an imitator, don't be just a carbon copy. Don't try to become a Buddha and don't try to become a Christ. Beware of books like Thomas à Kempis' book *Imitation of Christ* – beware. No imitation is going to help. The *vishuddha* is destroyed by noncreativity, imitation; and it is helped by creativity, expression, finding your own style of life, being courageous enough to "do your own thing." Art, song, music, dance, inventiveness are all helpful. But be inventive –

whatsoever you do, try to do it in a new way. Try to bring some individuality into it, bring some authentic signature. Even cleaning a floor, you can do it in your own way; even cooking food, you can do it in your own way. You can bring creativity to everything that you do; it should be brought. In as much as you are creative the *vishuddha* will open. And when the *vishuddha* opens, only then can the energy move into the *agya*, the third-eye center, the sixth center.

This is the process: first cleanse every center, purify it, beware of what damages it, and help it so that it becomes naturally functioning. Blocks are removed, energy rushes.

Beyond the sixth is the *sahasrar*, the *turiya*, the one-thousand-petaled lotus. You bloom. Yes, that's exactly what it is. Man is a tree: the *muladhar* is the root and *sahasrar* is the blooming of it. The flower has bloomed, your fragrance is released to the winds. That is the only prayer; that is the only offering to the feet of the divine. Borrowed flowers won't do, stolen flowers from the trees won't do; you have to flower and offer your flowers.

Now the sutras of Saraha. The first:

For the delights of kissing the deluded crave,
declaring it to be the ultimately real –
like a man who leaves his house and standing at the door
asks a woman for reports of sensual delights.

Kissing is symbolic – symbolic of any meeting between yin and yang, between male and female, between Shiva and Shakti. Whether you are holding hands with a woman – this is a kissing, hands kissing each other – or you are touching her lips with your lips, that is kissing; or your genital organs together – that too is a kiss. So the kiss is symbolic in Tantra of all meetings of opposite polarities. Sometimes you can kiss just by seeing a woman. If your eyes meet and touch each other there is a kiss, the meeting has happened.

For the delights of kissing the deluded crave, declaring it to be the ultimately real... Saraha says that the deluded – the people who are not alert at all to what they are doing – go on hankering for, missing, the other: man, the woman; woman, the man. They are continuously hankering to meet the other – and the meeting never happens. The absurdity of it is this: you hanker and hanker and desire and desire, and nothing but frustration comes into your hands. Saraha says this is not the ultimately real meeting. The ultimately real meeting is that which happens in the *sahasrar*. Once it has happened, it has happened forever. That is real. The meeting that happens outside is unreal, momentary, temporal – just a delusion.

It is *...like a man who leaves his house and standing at the door asks a woman for reports of sensual delights*. A beautiful simile. Saraha says that holding the hand of a woman outside, while the woman inside is waiting to be yours and forever yours, is just *...like a man who leaves his house and standing at the door asks a woman for reports of sensual delights*.

First *...leaves his house...* You are leaving your house, your innermost core, in search of a woman outside – and the woman is within. You will miss her wherever you go; you can go on running all over the earth and chasing all sorts of women and men. It is a mirage, it is a rainbow search, nothing comes into your hands. The woman is inside, and you are leaving the house.

And then *...standing at the door...* That too is symbolic. You are always standing at the door, by the senses – those are doors. Eyes are doors, hands are doors, genital organs are doors, ears are doors – these are doors. We are always standing at the door. Looking through the eyes, hearing through the ears, trying to touch with the hands, a man continuously remains at the door and forgets how to go inside the house. And then the absurdity of it – you don't know what love is and you ask a woman about the delights, about her experience. You think that by listening to her experience you will become blissful. It is taking the menu for the food.

Saraha is saying that first you go out of yourself – stand at the door – and then you ask others what delight is, what life is, what joy is, what God is. And God is waiting all the time within you. He resides in you, and you are asking others. And do you think that by listening to them you will come to any understanding?

The stirring of biotic forces in the house of nothingness
has given artificial rise to pleasures in so many ways.
Such yogis from affliction faint for they have fallen
from celestial space, inveigled into vice.

First: sex is not the ultimate in pleasure, it is just the beginning, the alpha, the *ABC* of it; it is not the omega. Sex is not the ultimately real, it is not the bliss supreme, but just an echo of it; the *sahasrar* is far away. When your sex center feels a little happiness, it is just a faraway echo of the *sahasrar*. The closer you come to the *sahasrar*, the more happiness you feel.

When you move from the *muladhar* to the *svadhishthan*, you feel happier – the first meeting of the *muladhar* and the *svadhishthan* is of great joy. Then the second meeting is of even greater joy. Then the third meeting and you cannot believe that more joy can be possible; but still more is possible because you are still far away – not very far but still at a distance – from the *sahasrar*. The *sahasrar* is just incredible. The bliss is so much that you are no more, only bliss is. The bliss is so much that you cannot say, "I am blissful," you simply know that you *are* bliss.

At the seventh you are just a tremor of joy – naturally so. Joy happens in the *sahasrar* and then it has to pass six layers. Much is lost, it is just an echo. Beware: don't mistake the echo for the real. Yes, even in the echo something of the real is there. Find the thread of reality in it. Catch hold of the thread and start moving inward.

The stirring of biotic forces in the house of nothingness has given artificial rise to pleasures in so many ways. And because of this delusion that sex is the ultimate in pleasure, so many artificial things have become very important. Money has become very important because you can purchase anything for money: you can purchase sex. Power has become important because through power you can have as much sex as you want; a poor man cannot afford it. Kings used to have thousands of wives – even in the twentieth century, the Nizam of Hyderabad had five hundred wives. Naturally, one who has power can have as much sex as he wants. Thousands of other problems have arisen because of this delusion that sex is the ultimately real: money, power, prestige.

The stirring of biotic forces in the house of nothingness... It is just imagination; it is just imagination that you are thinking it is pleasure. It is autohypnosis, autosuggestion. And once you autosuggest to yourself it looks like pleasure. Just think: holding the hand of a woman, and you feel such pleasure: it is just auto-hypnosis. It is just an idea in the mind.

The stirring of biotic forces... Because of this idea in the mind, your bioenergy is stirred. It is stirred sometimes even while looking at a *Playboy* picture; there is nobody, just lines and colors – and your energy can be stirred. Sometimes just an idea in the mind and your energy can be stirred. Energy follows imagination.

The stirring of biotic forces in the house of nothingness – you can create dreams, you can project dreams onto the screen of noth-ingness – has given artificial rise to pleasures in so many ways.

If you watch the pathology of man, you will be amazed: people have such ideas that you cannot believe what is hap-pening. Some man cannot make love to his woman unless he looks at pornography first. The real seems to be less real than the unreal; he becomes excited only through the unreal. Have you not seen it again and again in your own life that the real seems to be less exciting than the unreal?

Remember to change your consciousness from the imaginary to the real. Always listen to the real. Unless you are very, very alert you will remain in the trap of the imaginary.

The imaginary seems to be very satisfying for many reasons. It is under your control. You can have my nose as long as you want – in your imagination. You can think whatsoever you want to think; nobody can hinder it, nobody can enter your imagination, you are utterly free. You can paint me as you want, you can imagine me, you can expect, you can make whatsoever you want of me. You are free; the ego feels very good.

That's why when a master is dead he finds more disciples than while he is alive. With a dead master, disciples are completely at ease; with a living master, they are in difficulty. Buddha never had as many disciples as he has now, after twenty-five centuries. Jesus had only twelve disciples; now, half of the earth. Just see the impact of the absent master: now Jesus is in your hands, you can do whatsoever you want to do with him. He is no longer alive, he cannot destroy your dreams and imaginations. If the so-called Christians had seen the real Jesus, their hearts would stop fluttering immediately. Why? – because they would not believe. They have imagined things, and Jesus is a real man. You could have found him in a pub, drinking with friends and gossiping. Now, this doesn't look like the "only begotten son of God." It looks very ordinary: maybe he is just the carpenter Joseph's son. But once Jesus is gone, he cannot interfere with your imagination. Then you can picture and paint and create images of him as you like.

Far away it is easier: the imagination has full power. The closer you come to me, the less and less power your imagination will have. And you will never be able to see me unless you drop your imagination. So is the case with all other pleasures.

The stirring of biotic forces in the house of nothingness has given artificial rise to pleasures in so many ways. Such yogis from affliction faint for they have fallen from celestial space, inveigled into vice. If you imagine too much, you will lose your celestial space. Imagination is samsara, imagination is your dream. If you dream too much, you will lose the celestial space, you will lose your divinity, you will not be a conscious being. Imagination will outweigh you, it will overburden you, you will be lost in a fantasy. You can faint in your fantasy and you can think that it is *samadhi*. There are people who faint and then they think they are in *samadhi*. Buddha has called such *samadhis* "wrong *samadhis*." So too Saraha says that it is a wrong *samadhi*. Imagining about God, going on into your imagination, feeding your imagination, nurturing it more and more, fantasizing more and more – you will faint, you will lose all consciousness; you will have beautiful dreams of your own creation.

But this is falling from the celestial space. And Saraha says that to fall from your purity of awareness is the only vice. What does he mean by the "celestial space"? Space without any dreams. Dreaming is the world; without dreaming you are in nirvana.

> *As a brahmin, who with rice and butter*
> *makes a burned offering in blazing fire*
> *creating a vessel for nectar from celestial space,*
> *takes this, through wishful thinking, as the ultimate.*

In India, the brahmins have been doing *yagnas*. They have been offering rice and butter to the fire, the blazing fire, and imagining that the offering is going to God. Sitting around a fire, fasting for many days, doing certain rituals, certain mantras, repeating certain scriptures, you can create a state of autohypnosis. You can be fooled by yourself and you can think that you are reaching God.

Saraha says that those who really want to enter godliness will have to burn their inner fire; the outer fire won't do. And those who really want to attain will have to burn their own seeds of desire; rice won't do. And those who really want to attain will have to burn their ego; butter won't do. Butter is just the most essential part of milk, the most purified part of milk. So is ego the most purified dream; it is ghee, purified butter. Offering ghee to the fire is not going to help. You have to burn your inner fire.

And sexual energy moving upward becomes a fire, it becomes a flame. It is fire! Even when it moves outward, it gives birth to life; sex energy is the most miraculous thing. It is through sex energy that life is born. Life is fire, it is a function of fire; without fire, life cannot exist. Without the sun there will be no trees, no men, no birds, no animals. It is transformed fire that becomes life.

While making love to a woman, the fire is going outward. While moving inward, the fire is going in. And when you throw your seeds of desire, seeds of thought, seeds of ambition, seeds of greed into this fire, they are burned. And then, finally, you throw your ego – the most purified dream; that too is burned. This is real *yagna*, real ritual, real sacrifice.

As a brahmin who with rice and butter makes a burned offering in blazing fire creating a vessel for nectar from celestial space, takes this, through wishful thinking, as the ultimate. And he thinks, through wishful thinking, that this is the ultimate. The man who is making love to a woman and thinks that it is the ultimate is throwing into the outer fire in exactly the same way; he is pouring into something outside. And so is the woman who thinks she is making love or moving into a great space of bliss and benediction by just making love to a man, just throwing out her fire.

The fire has to move inward; then it gives a rebirth to you, it rejuvenates you.

Some people, who have kindled the inner heat
and raised it to the fontanel,
stroke the uvula with the tongue in a sort of coition
and confuse that which fetters with what gives release,
in pride will call themselves yogis.

And a very important thing: just as I explained to you the map, you have to remember that the *vishuddha*, the fifth chakra, is in the throat. *Vishuddha*, the throat chakra, is the last point from which you can fall. Up to that point there is a possibility of falling back. With the sixth chakra, the third eye, attained, there is no possibility of falling back. You have gone beyond the point from which one can return. The point of no return is the third eye. If you die at the third-eye center, you will be born at the third-eye center. If you die at the *sahasrar*, you will not be born again. But if you die at the *vishuddha*, you will slip back to the first, the *muladhar*. In the next life you will have to start from the *muladhar* again.

So up to the fifth there is no certainty; there is promise, but no certainty. Up to the fifth there is every possibility of falling back. And one of the greatest possibilities that has caused many people in India to fall back is, this sutra says: *Some people, who have kindled the inner heat and raised it to the fontanel...*

You can create the inner heat – the flame starts moving upward and it comes to the throat; then there arises a great desire to tickle the throat with the tongue. Beware of it. In India they have devised great techniques for tickling it with the tongue. They have even cut the roots of the tongue so that the tongue becomes long and can easily move backward – you will find many yogis doing that. The tongue can move backward and it can tickle the fifth center. That tickling is masturbatory because the sex energy has come there.

Just as I told you, the fifth chakra, *vishuddha*, is male. When the male energy comes to the throat, your throat becomes almost a genital organ – of more superiority, of more finesse than the genital organ. Just a little tickle with the tongue and you enjoy greatly. But that is masturbatory, and once you start doing that... And it is very, very great pleasure, sex is nothing compared to it. Remember it: sex is just nothing compared to it. Tickling with your own tongue, you can enjoy it so much. So in yoga there are methods...

Saraha is making it clear that no Tantrika should do that. It is a deception and a great failure because the energy has come up to the fifth, and now the desire arises to tickle it; that is the last desire. If you can keep yourself alert and can move beyond that desire, then you will reach the sixth center, the *agya*; otherwise you will start falling back. That is the last temptation. In fact, in Tantra that is the temptation which you can say that Jesus had when Satan came and tempted him, or Buddha had when Mara came and tempted him. This is the last temptation, the last effort of your desire-mind, the last effort of your dream world, the last effort of the ego before it is lost utterly. It makes a last effort to tempt you. And the temptation is really great: it is very difficult to avoid it. It is so pleasurable, infinitely more pleasurable than sex pleasure.

When people think that sex pleasure is the ultimate, what to say about this pleasure? And it loses no energy. In sex you have to lose energy; you feel frustrated, tired, weak. But if you tickle your sex energy when it has come to the throat, there is no loss of energy. And you can go on tickling the whole day – that's what Jose Delgado has attained through mechanical devices.

Some people, who have kindled the inner heat and raised it to the fontanel, stroke the uvula with the tongue in a sort of coition and confuse that which fetters with that which gives release… This is again samsara – falling back into samsara. …and confuse that which fetters with that which gives release, in pride will call themselves yogis. But they are not, they have missed. In fact the right word for them is yogabrashta, "one who has fallen from yoga."

The fifth center is the most dangerous center. You cannot tickle any other center – that is the danger of it. You cannot tickle the *swadhishthan*, you cannot tickle the *manipura*, you cannot tickle the *anahata*; they are beyond you, there is no way to reach them and tickle them. You cannot tickle the third eye. The only point which can be tickled is the *vishuddha*, your throat center, because it is available. The mouth is open, it is available, and the easiest way is to turn your tongue backward and tickle it.

In yoga treatises you will find it described as something great; it is not, beware of it.

This is the inner map of Tantra alchemy. The energy can start moving any time; you just have to bring to your lovemaking a little meditation, a little inwardness. Tantra is not against lovemaking, remember; let it be repeated again and again. It is all for it, but not just for it; it is the first rung of the ladder, a seven-runged ladder.

Man is a ladder. The first rung is sex and the seventh rung is the *sahasrar – samadhi*. The first rung joins you with samsara, the world, and the seventh rung joins you with nirvana, the beyond. With the first rung, you move in a vicious circle of birth and death again and again; it is repetitive. With the seventh rung, you go beyond birth and death. Life eternal is yours – the kingdom of God.

PART III

CHAKRA MEDITATIONS

CHAPTER 11

OSHO Chakra Breathing Meditation

This active meditation uses deep, rapid breathing and body movement to open and bring awareness, vitality and silence to each of the seven chakras* and thus into your life.

The accompanying music and bells energetically support the process and indicate the beginning of each stage. The meditation is best done on an empty stomach.

* All chakras lie deep within, rather than on the surface of the body. The following "map" is used to indicate their approximate locations:
   1. base chakra: the sex center, lower pelvis
   2. sacral chakra: just below the navel
   3. solar plexus chakra: above the navel, below the breastbone
   4. heart chakra: the middle of the chest
   5. throat chakra: the throat
   6. third-eye chakra: between the eyebrows
   7. crown chakra: top of the head

This meditation is to be done with its specific OSHO Chakra Breathing Meditation music, which indicates and energetically supports the different stages.

INSTRUCTIONS
The meditation lasts one hour and has two stages. Keep your eyes closed throughout.

FIRST STAGE: 45 MINUTES
Stand with your feet a little apart, your body loose and relaxed. Close your eyes and with open mouth breathe deeply and rapidly into the first chakra – your attention with each breath in the pelvic area, where the first chakra is located. Have equal emphasis on the in and the out breath. Don't force your breathing, breathe in a rhythm that feels comfortable and allows you to become aware of the feelings and sensations of each chakra.

Each time you hear a bell, move this deep, rapid breathing up to the next chakra. As you breathe up from chakra to chakra, let your breathing become more rapid and gentler, so that you are taking about twice as many breaths in the seventh chakra than in the first.

To support the breathing you can shake, stretch, rotate or move your body and hands as you feel, but let your feet stay in one spot. Allow your feet, knees, hips and other joints to become like springs so that once you set the breathing and body in motion, the movement will become continuous and effortless. Let your awareness remain primarily with the sensations of the chakras, rather than with the breathing or the body movement.

After breathing in the seventh chakra, you will hear three bells. Now let your breath and awareness turn and fall back down through each chakra, allowing your breath to become slower from chakra to chakra. Let the energy flow down by itself to include the entire spectrum of chakra energy from top to bottom, like seven colors blending into one rainbow. You have about two minutes to reach back to the first chakra and it is up to you how long you breathe into each chakra.

After you finish this sequence, stand silently for a few moments before starting the next sequence. This upward and downward breathing sequence is repeated three times.

If at first you don't feel the energy of your chakras, just breathe into the area where they are located. Remember not to push the breath – rather allow the breath and body movement to be like a bridge carrying you into the sensations and energy qualities of each chakra. Becoming sensitive to this comes through awareness and patience.

SECOND STAGE: 15 MINUTES
After the third breathing sequence, sit relaxed and in silence. Remain a witness to whatever is happening within, without judgment.

CHAPTER 12

OSHO Chakra Sounds Meditation

This meditation can be done at any time. It uses vocal sounds to open and harmonize the chakras* or energy centers while bringing awareness to them. It can bring you into a deep, peaceful, inner silence either through making your own vocal sounds or by just listening to the music and feeling the sounds within you.

* All chakras lie deep within, rather than on the surface of the body. The following "map" is used to indicate their approximate locations:

1. base chakra: the sex center, lower pelvis
2. sacral chakra: just below the navel
3. solar plexus chakra: above the navel, below the breastbone
4. heart chakra: the middle of the chest
5. throat chakra: the throat
6. third-eye chakra: between the eyebrows
7. crown chakra: top of the head

This meditation is to be done with its specific OSHO Chakra Sounds Meditation music, which indicates and energetically supports the different stages.

INSTRUCTIONS

The meditation lasts one hour and has two stages. Keep your eyes closed throughout.

FIRST STAGE: 45 MINUTES

Stand, sit comfortably, or lie down if you prefer. Keep your back straight and your body loose. Breathe into your belly rather than your chest. The sounds should be made with your mouth open and your jaw loose, keeping your mouth open the whole time. Close your eyes and listen to the music; if you wish, start making sounds in the first chakra. You can make a single tone or you can vary the tone. Let the music guide you; however, you can be creative with your own sounds. While listening to the sound of the music or the sounds that you make, feel the sounds pulsating in the very center of the chakra, even if it seems to be imagination at first.

Imagination can be used for "becoming attuned to something that is already there." So keep doing the meditation even if it feels like you may be imagining the chakras. With awareness, your imagination can lead you to an experience of the inner vibrations of each center.

After making sounds in the first chakra, you will hear the tones change to a higher pitch – this is the indication to listen and feel sounds in the second chakra. If you wish, you can continue making sounds also. This process is repeated all the way up to the seventh chakra. As you move from chakra to chakra, let your sounds become higher in pitch.

After listening to and making sounds in the seventh chakra, the tones will descend one at a time down through all the chakras. As you hear the tones go down, listen and make sounds in each chakra. Feel the inside of your body becoming hollow like a bamboo flute, allowing the sounds to resonate from the top of your head down to the very base of your trunk.

At the end of the sequence, you will hear a pause before the next sequence starts. This upward and downward movement of sound will be repeated three times for a total of 45 minutes.

After you have become familiar with the meditation, you can add another dimension to it through visualization – allowing visual images to appear in your imagination as you focus on each chakra. There is no need to create images, just be receptive to any which may come. The images could be colors, patterns, or scenes of nature. What comes to your awareness may be visual, or it may come as a thought – for example, you may think "gold" or you may see color in your imagination.

SECOND STAGE: 15 MINUTES
After the last sound sequence, sit or lie down with closed eyes. Remain in silence and don't focus on anything in particular. Become aware of and watch whatever is happening within – relaxed, without any judgment, remaining a witness.

Music is a very subtle meditation. The seven notes of music are concerned with the seven chakras of the body and each chakra has its own note. If you concentrate on that chakra, you will start hearing that note arising within your body. The second chakra has two notes, the third, three. One is important, the other two are just part of it but create a harmony. It goes on becoming a greater harmony, rising higher with each chakra. On the seventh chakra it is an orchestra.

Each chakra has its own form, its own music, its own taste, its own smell. The deeper you move inside yourself, the more you find the whole world because if it is not within you, you cannot see it without either. Something is needed to correspond.

CHAPTER 13

Online Resources

YOUR MOST IMPORTANT WEB LINKS

Audio and video instructions for the OSHO Active Meditations and other OSHO Meditations are given on osho.com/meditation and on imeditate.osho.com. For live participation options from your home, log in on: imeditate.osho.com.

About Osho

Osho's unique contribution to the understanding of who we are defies categorization. Mystic and scientist, a rebellious spirit whose sole interest is to alert humanity to the urgent need to discover a new way of living. To continue as before is to invite threats to our very survival on this unique and beautiful planet.

His essential point is that only by changing ourselves, one individual at a time, can the outcome of all our "selves" – our societies, our cultures, our beliefs, our world – also change. The doorway to that change is meditation.

Osho the scientist has experimented and scrutinized all the approaches of the past and examined their effects on the modern human being and responded to their shortcomings by creating a new starting point for the hyperactive 21st Century mind: OSHO Active Meditations.

Once the agitation of a modern lifetime has started to settle, "activity" can melt into "passivity" a key starting point of real meditation. To support this next step, Osho has transformed the ancient "art of listening" into a subtle contemporary methodology: the OSHO Talks. Here words become music, the listener discovers who is listening, and the awareness moves from what is being heard to the individual doing the listening. Magically, as silence arises, what needs to be heard is understood directly, free from the distraction of a mind that can only interrupt and interfere with this delicate process.

These thousands of talks cover everything from the individual quest for meaning to the most urgent social and political issues facing society today. Osho's books are not written but are transcribed from audio and video recordings of these

extemporaneous talks to international audiences. As he puts it, "So remember: whatever I am saying is not just for you... I am talking also for the future generations."

Osho has been described by *The Sunday Times* in London as one of the "1000 Makers of the 20th Century" and by American author Tom Robbins as "the most dangerous man since Jesus Christ." *Sunday Mid-Day* (India) has selected Osho as one of ten people – along with Gandhi, Nehru and Buddha – who have changed the destiny of India.

About his own work Osho has said that he is helping to create the conditions for the birth of a new kind of human being. He often characterizes this new human being as "Zorba the Buddha" – capable both of enjoying the earthy pleasures of a Zorba the Greek and the silent serenity of a Gautama the Buddha.

Running like a thread through all aspects of Osho's talks and meditations is a vision that encompasses both the timeless wisdom of all ages past and the highest potential of today's (and tomorrow's) science and technology.

Osho is known for his revolutionary contribution to the science of inner transformation, with an approach to meditation that acknowledges the accelerated pace of contemporary life. His unique OSHO Active Meditations™ are designed to first release the accumulated stresses of body and mind, so that it is then easier to take an experience of stillness and thought-free relaxation into daily life.

Two autobiographical works by the author are available:
Autobiography of a Spiritually Incorrect Mystic,
St Martins Press, New York (book and eBook)
Glimpses of a Golden Childhood,
OSHO Media International, Pune, India

OSHO International Meditation Resort

Each year the Meditation Resort welcomes thousands of people from more than 100 countries. The unique campus provides an opportunity for a direct personal experience of a new way of living – with more awareness, relaxation, celebration and creativity. A great variety of around-the-clock and around-the-year program options are available. Doing nothing and just relaxing is one of them!

All of the programs are based on Osho's vision of "Zorba the Buddha" – a qualitatively new kind of human being who is able *both* to participate creatively in everyday life *and* to relax into silence and meditation.

Location
Located 100 miles southeast of Mumbai in the thriving modern city of Pune, India, the OSHO International Medi-tation Resort is a holiday destination with a difference. The Meditation Resort is spread over 28 acres of spectacular gardens in a beautiful tree-lined residential area.

OSHO Meditations
A full daily schedule of meditations for every type of person includes both traditional and revolutionary methods, and particularly the OSHO Active Meditations™. The daily meditation program takes place in what must be the world's largest meditation hall, the OSHO Auditorium.

OSHO Multiversity

Individual sessions, courses and workshops cover everything from creative arts to holistic health, personal transformation, relationship and life transition, transforming meditation into a lifestyle for life and work, esoteric sciences, and the "Zen" approach to sports and recreation. The secret of the OSHO Multiversity's success lies in the fact that all its programs are combined with meditation, supporting the understanding that as human beings we are far more than the sum of our parts.

OSHO Basho Spa

The luxurious Basho Spa provides for leisurely open-air swimming surrounded by trees and tropical green. The uniquely styled, spacious Jacuzzi, the saunas, gym, tennis courts…all these are enhanced by their stunningly beautiful setting.

Cuisine

A variety of different eating areas serve delicious Western, Asian and Indian vegetarian food – most of it organically grown especially for the Meditation Resort. Breads and cakes are baked in the resort's own bakery.

Night life

There are many evening events to choose from – dancing being at the top of the list! Other activities include full-moon meditations beneath the stars, variety shows, music performances and meditations for daily life.

Facilities

You can buy all of your basic necessities and toiletries in the Galleria. The Multimedia Gallery sells a large range of OSHO media products. There is also a bank, a travel agency and a Cyber Café on-campus. For those who enjoy shopping, Pune provides all the options, ranging from traditional and ethnic

Indian products to all of the global brand-name stores.

Accommodation
You can choose to stay in the elegant rooms of the OSHO Guest-house, or for longer stays on campus you can select one of the OSHO Living-In programs. Additionally there is a plentiful variety of nearby hotels and serviced apartments.

www.osho.com/meditationresort
www.osho.com/guesthouse
www.osho.com/livingin

For More Information

www. **OSHO** .com

a comprehensive multi-language website including a magazine, OSHO Books, OSHO Talks in audio and video formats, the OSHO Library text archive in English and Hindi and extensive information about OSHO Meditations. You will also find the program schedule of the OSHO Multiversity and information about the OSHO International Meditation Resort.

http://OSHO.com/AllAboutOSHO
http://OSHO.com/Resort
http://OSHO.com/Shop
http://www.youtube.com/OSHO
http://www.Twitter.com/OSHO
http://www.facebook.com/pages/OSHO.International

To contact OSHO International Foundation:
www.osho.com/oshointernational,
oshointernational@oshointernational.com